Presented to:

_____

From:

_____

Date:

_____

101 Amazing Things God Thinks About You

*Discover Your God-given
Purpose and Identity*

David C Cook

transforming lives together

101 AMAZING THINGS GOD THINKS ABOUT YOU
Published by David C. Cook
4050 Lee Vance View
Colorado Springs, CO 80918 U.S.A.

David C. Cook Distribution Canada
55 Woodslee Avenue, Paris, Ontario, Canada N3L 3E5

David C. Cook U.K., Kingsway Communications
Eastbourne, East Sussex BN23 6NT, England

David C. Cook and the graphic circle C logo
are registered trademarks of Cook Communications Ministries.

ISBN 978-1-56292-229-0

© 2004 Bordon Books
Manuscript written by Vicki Kuyper
Developed by Bordon Books
6532 E. 71st Street, Suite 105
Tulsa, OK 74133

Printed in the United States of America
First Edition 2004

6 7 8 9 10 11 12 13

070210

Introduction

Before you were born, God thought about who you would be, what you would look like, and what your purpose in life would be. He also thought about every moment of your life and, even more amazing, He now thinks about every moment of your eternity with Him!

With all that divine thought headed in your direction, wouldn't you like to know some of the things God is thinking about you? You can! The Bible is filled with all kinds of information that not only tells you what God thinks about you, but also how He feels about you. Paul told the believers at Ephesus that he wanted them to know the height, length, and depth of God's love for them. He knew that if they understood how big God's love for them was, their lives would be transformed. Yours will be too.

Turn the pages and find out *101 Amazing Things God Thinks About You.* Your life will change and you will never think about yourself in the same way again.

1.
God knew you before you were born!

Sometimes you may find it hard to believe that the God of the universe knows where you live and how you feel about your life. But God has made it His business to know you so well that He knew you before you even entered your mother's womb.

Think about that: God knew your name, your likes and dislikes, your temperament, your hair color, even your deepest desire, all before your conception.

So the next time you feel too small for God to concern himself about you, remember that when you were a sparkle in your father's eye, your Heavenly Father already knew you and took the time to remember everything about you. He loves you that much.

"BEFORE I FORMED YOU IN THE WOMB I KNEW YOU."
JEREMIAH 1:5 NIV

2.
Jesus prayed for you in the Garden of Gethsemane.

Wouldn't you like to know what God prayed for you? You can. Just look in the prayer Jesus prayed in the Garden of Gethsemane on the night He was arrested. He prayed that you would be as close to Him as He was to God. Wouldn't you like to feel that close to God? Jesus wants that too. And if Jesus prayed for it, don't you think God will answer it?

And He also prayed that you would get along with other believers so that your relationship with them would be as close as the one He has with God the Father and one filled with peace and agreement. Think about the relationships you have with other believers. Are there some areas where things could be "friendlier"? Why not ask God for help in repairing those relationships. God has prayed that you would be at peace, so you can be assured you will have His help and guidance.

What was the final thing Jesus asked God to give Him concerning you? He said, "Father, I want those you have given me to be with me where I am, and to see my glory, the glory you have given me because you loved me before the creation of the world" (John 17:24 NIV). Jesus wants you to be close to Him in

Heaven and to see Him as He really is. He doesn't want to keep a thing from you about himself. So when you wonder what Jesus was really like, you can know that He is eager to tell you about himself both now and in Heaven. Read about His life in the Gospels and then don't be afraid to ask Him questions about what it was like to be the Son of God in a small town. He will answer you—if not now, then later, when you see Him in Heaven.

"I PRAY ALSO FOR THOSE WHO WILL BELIEVE
IN ME THROUGH THEIR MESSAGE."
JOHN 17:20 NIV

3.
You are not subject to any man's judgement!

One of the hardest things about life is realizing the number of times we are evaluated. From the time we are born and the doctor scores us on the Apgar scale of 0-10, to the time we graduate with a file cabinet full of papers with grades on them and all through our lives, people judge us and tell us what they think of us. But God says that as a believer you are not subject to any person's judgement. Why? Part of the reason is that most of the people who are trying to judge you will be attempting to evaluate you without the help of a renewed mind.

When you become a Christian, you are given a new mind (See fact #5!) which changes how you see the world around you and the people in it. That new mind has been rescued from spiritual darkness, and the lies that the world suffers from no longer have the power to fool you. So when you do something according to the truth that God has shown you in His Word, it makes no sense to those who do not have your new mind. They can't judge you because they have blurred vision from the spiritual darkness that holds them captive.

Also you have someone living inside you to coach you so that your judgement is truer than it was before you met Jesus. That someone is the Holy Spirit. So you may see what is truly happening in the world and in your life, but others who do not have the help of God cannot understand what they see. Their judgement is faulty.

Knowing that God doesn't think you need to worry about their opinion should help you to let yourself off the hook when you are criticized for doing what is right. God understands the thinking handicap they suffer from. And it also means that you can understand and love them, even while they are hostile. You know that they need help—Jesus' help.

So next time someone judges you, remember—you are not subject to their judgement, and you can love them and pray for them because they can't help being wrong right now.

THE SPIRITUAL MAN MAKES JUDGEMENTS ABOUT ALL
THINGS, BUT HE HIMSELF IS NOT SUBJECT TO ANY
MAN'S JUDGMENT.
1 CORINTHIANS 2:15 NIV

4.
You are dead!

Funny! You don't feel dead, do you? So what is this all about? If you are a believer, God says that you have died with Christ. When you are baptized and go down into the water, that action symbolized your burial with Jesus when He died. So every believer can say, "I'm dead with Christ."

But that isn't the end of the story. When you came back up out of the water, that action symbolized your part in His resurrection, His coming back to life. God says that your old self remains dead, and a new self created by God and indwelt by God's Spirit is what comes up out of the water. (See Romans 6:3-4.)

This truth makes all the difference to you in your battle to do what is right day by day. You can ignore those screams you hear inside when a part of you protests and wants to go the wrong way. The old self says things such as, "Hey, I can't do that—it's too hard. I won't be happy. You are killing me!"

But you are not killing the old self—it is already dead. God says you can treat that part as though it has died because He has given you power over it.

That is not the same as mistreating yourself. God loves you and would never want you to do what is wrong—even to yourself. This is more like giving the best part of yourself the power to decide what you do and ignoring the part of yourself that tries to get your attention and to convince you to go astray.

So the old you is dead and the new you is in charge. Think about that the next time there is a fight inside, and let the new you decide what goes.

"I HAVE BEEN CRUCIFIED WITH CHRIST
AND I NO LONGER LIVE."
GALATIANS 2:20 NIV

5.
You have a new mind!

It takes a new mind to be able to see what God is doing. And it takes a new mind to be able to think that what He is doing is a good thing. As humans we are born into a world that has fallen away from the truth, and we live in a spiritual darkness without realizing it.

When we begin to see that we are in need of God's forgiveness and that we need Him, a kind of miracle has taken place inside us. When we ask Jesus to come into our lives and to dwell inside us, another miracle has taken place. In both cases, the miracle is being able to see clearly what is true about ourselves and God as well as being able to see that this truth is a good thing, that God himself is good. These abilities come from having been given a new mind.

But that is not the end of the story. God does not make a habit of taking over people's minds, so He opens our eyes enough to get us started. Then He calls us to take actions through which our mind changes even more for the better. A Christian will want to do the things that will cause the most change inside, such as reading the Bible. Another action we can take is to spend time with God because our mental fogginess dissipates around Him. He is truth, and the truth shines when you are with Him.

God tells us that we need to keep working to get out from under the spiritual fog that the world creates. Paul wrote, "Do not be conformed to this world, but be transformed by the renewing of your mind, so that you may prove what the will of God is, that which is good and acceptable and perfect" (Romans 12:2 NASB).

Note the last half of that verse: If your mind is renewed, you will be able to see that everything that God does is good, acceptable to you, and perfect. It is a miracle to see the truth. And it is another miracle to see that God is good, even when you have to go through some things that are hard.

So . . . you have a new mind. Why not begin today to shine it up even more by doing the things that dispel the remaining fog?

WE HAVE THE MIND OF CHRIST.
1 CORINTHIANS 2:16 NIV

6.
You are possessed!

"Whoa!" you say. "I've seen those horror films and heard stories about that. I'm nowhere near possessed."

No? Well, let's talk about that. When we read about accounts of possession in the Gospels, Jesus sets people free who are held captive by the devil. They are indwelled by an evil spirit that is loyal to the devil, and they suffer from a loss of freedom. They can't do what they want to do; and this spirit, who delights in tormenting them, abuses them. So, no, you are correct in thinking that you are not possessed by an evil spirit.

But let's think about how God made you. You may not realize it, but you were designed to be indwelled by God's Spirit. It is a bit like being a battery-driven device. Just because someone puts the wrong battery into a device and it doesn't operate doesn't mean that the device was meant to run without any batteries at all.

Before we were in Christ, it was as if we were running without batteries. The physical and mental parts of our being ran on food, water, and oxygen, but the spiritual part was not running at all. Some people, such as the ones we see in the Gospels, have experienced the torment of having the wrong battery inside them. When they accepted Christ, He removed the wrong battery and healed them. That is what we see in the Gospels, and we call it being delivered from an evil spirit.

But in Acts we see a special event in which God's Spirit comes to dwell inside the disciples, and Christians from that time have been taught to expect to experience the Holy Spirit helping them as a part of the new life.

"But I can't feel anything," you say. "I don't feel possessed."

That is because God loves you. And He loves your freedom to decide whether you will seek Him and spend time with Him. He wants a relationship that is healthy and real between you and Him. That requires that you be free to choose. You could say that His hand is very light on your spiritual shoulder. He suggests, but He never overpowers you against your will.

Even so, you are designed to be indwelled by God, and you either belong to God's enemy or to Him. The choices are limited.

However, if you were to read the journals and biographies of Christians who embraced God's lordship, you would find a surprising thing. None of them feel trapped, or mistreated, or deprived in any way. To them the choice is wide open and wonderful—they get God. To them, He is the great treasure worth more than anything the world offers.

You really were designed not only to be indwelled by God so that you could be as close to Him as Jesus is to the Father, but you were designed to get the most supreme pleasure out of that relationship. God knows this, and that is why He doesn't apologize for His call for obedience and worship. He knows we will be supremely happy when we give up the lesser joys offered by the world and discover the true joy that is found when we give ourselves to Him without reservation.

You are possessed by God, who is head over heels in love with you—and it is a good thing.

DO YOU NOT KNOW THAT YOUR BODY IS A TEMPLE OF THE HOLY SPIRIT WHO IS IN YOU, WHOM YOU HAVE FROM GOD, AND THAT YOU ARE NOT YOUR OWN?
1 CORINTHIANS 6:19 NASB

7.
You are designed to have God as your GPS.

Forget maps, road atlases, and asking for directions at the nearest service station. Today you can purchase a vehicle with a Global Positioning System (GPS). Just key in your destination and this handy little device will guide you to your objective, via the most time-efficient route. With the help of a satellite, you can not only chart a route to where you're going, but you can pinpoint exactly where you are right now. You'll never be lost again. Well, at least not while you're behind the wheel.

But finding your way in life can be a bit more difficult. That's why God offers you His very own GPS as standard equipment when you turn your life over to Him. The best part is that this guidance system never wears out or needs repair. All you have to do is choose to use it.

It's a three-part system that utilizes the Bible, the counsel of others, and God's Spirit. When you're faced with a decision, and are unsure of which way to turn, first take time out to pray. Ask God to give you the wisdom you need to make a decision that will honor Him. Then take time to read God's Word. It holds some basic rules about what's right and loving—and what's wrong and self-serving. Weigh your decision against what God has said in black and white.

If you're still unsure of which direction to go, turn to someone you respect, someone who you feel has a strong relationship with God. Ask for their input on the situation. Then go back to step one. Pray about all the counsel you've received, and ask God to clearly lead you in the direction you should go.

Unlike the GPS on your car, you may not be able to see where this decision will ultimately lead. But God knows. He's not only more reliable than a satellite, but on a very personal level He's infinitely more interested in your destination, as well as every inch of your journey. He cares that you arrive safely. So follow God's direction, one turn at a time. He'll get you where you need to go.

GOD CHARTS THE ROAD YOU TAKE.
PSALM 1:6 MSG

8.
You make Him sing.

Picture this. It's the middle of the night. The house is quiet, except for a melodically soothing sound coming from the nursery. There, a new mother rocks back and forth, singing a song of love over her precious newborn.

Now tweak that picture a bit. Change the image of the mother to that of your Heavenly Father. Then put yourself in the baby's place.

Far-fetched? Not at all. The Bible says that God will "rejoice over you with singing." Can you imagine what that will be like? To hear God's voice lilting with love and delight—because of you?

The next time you're feeling lonely, in need of comfort or encouragement, picture yourself in God's arms as He rejoices over you in song. Then, sing a love song to Him in return.

"THE LORD YOUR GOD IS WITH YOU, HE IS
MIGHTY TO SAVE. HE WILL TAKE GREAT DELIGHT
IN YOU, HE WILL QUIET YOU WITH HIS LOVE,
HE WILL REJOICE OVER YOU WITH SINGING."
ZEPHANIAH 3:17 NIV

9.
You may have met an angel face-to-face.

Angels are not just a decoration for the top of a Christmas tree or a cute little image to pin on your lapel. Angels are warriors. They are angelic beings that not only share Heaven with God but move about the earth doing His will. The Bible says that they help answer prayer, convey God's messages, offer protection, and sing praises to God.

The Bible also tells us that angels can move about unseen, show themselves as they really are, or even take human form. People like Abraham and Sarah, Jacob, and Lot all met angels face-to-face. You may have too, but chances are you didn't realize it.

Keep that in mind the next time you cross paths with a stranger. You never know when one of God's messengers may show up, unannounced, at your door.

DON'T FORGET TO SHOW HOSPITALITY TO STRANGERS,
FOR SOME WHO HAVE DONE THIS HAVE ENTERTAINED
ANGELS WITHOUT REALIZING IT!
HEBREWS 13:2 NLT

10.
You are a superstar.

Celebrities stand out. There is something about them that seems to be special, out of the ordinary. It may be incredible talent or jaw-dropping physical beauty. (Both of which happen to be gifts that come straight from the hand of God!) Or perhaps it's the novelty of their opulent or outrageous lifestyle. Whatever it is, their superstar status seems to guarantee center stage in the company of folks like the rest of us.

But believe it or not, you are a bonafide superstar. Something about you will draw others to you, something that makes you shine like a bright star in a midnight sky. That something is the Word of God alive in you. The darker—or farther away from God—the lives of those around you are, the brighter you'll shine. Like a living, breathing North Star, your life can point others in the right direction. Not toward you (shining as you are!) but toward God.

YOU SHINE LIKE STARS IN THE UNIVERSE
AS YOU HOLD OUT THE WORD OF LIFE.
PHILIPPIANS 2:15–16 NIV

11.
You've had a heart transplant.

Although an electrocardiogram would never have diagnosed it, you once had a heart of stone. That does not mean you were cold and "heartless." It simply means you weren't yet fully alive. Your heart wasn't moving in rhythm with God's own.

But once you put your life into God's hands, you not only receive a new destiny, but a brand-new heart—one made of flesh, not rock. While a stone just rests there, inflexible and immovable, flesh moves and grows and feels. It also bleeds. The closer you get to God, the more you'll notice that what breaks His heart will break yours as well. Poverty, betrayal, abuse, injustice . . . a tender heart of flesh cannot remain unmoved when it encounters situations such as these. Instead, it will be compelled to take action, even if that action is as simple—and powerful—as a heartfelt prayer.

"I WILL GIVE YOU A NEW HEART AND PUT A NEW SPIRIT IN YOU; I WILL REMOVE FROM YOU YOUR HEART OF STONE AND GIVE YOU A HEART OF FLESH."
EZEKIEL 36:26 NIV

12.
A ransom has been paid for your life.

Kidnappers, cryptic notes, and a briefcase full of cash . . . those are the kinds of images the word "ransom" may bring to mind.

But chances are you've never been in a real ransom situation. Or, at least, you never realized you were.

The truth is, God paid a high price to ransom you from death. The price wasn't paid in unmarked bills. Your life was traded for the life of God's only Son. Christ's agonizing death on the Cross and separation from His Heavenly Father was the only price high enough to set you free.

The only reason people agree to pay a ransom is because what or who is being held captive is valuable to them. You are immeasurably valuable to God. Your worth has been proven by the high price He paid. Why not take a moment right now and thank Him for what He's done on your behalf.

"DO NOT BE AFRAID, FOR I HAVE RANSOMED YOU. I
HAVE CALLED YOU BY NAME; YOU ARE MINE."
ISAIAH 43:1 NLT

13.
You can embrace others with your words.

Words have power. They can hurt or they can heal, chafe or soothe, divide or unite. They can profess your faith in God or reject Him as Savior. Your words can change the lives of those around you—as well as your own. What kind of difference will you make today?

The Bible says that what we say reveals what our hearts are really like. If you want to know yourself better, listen to what comes out of your mouth. Is it honest? Is it loving? Does it honor God? Does it draw others to you or push them away?

Sometimes, honesty requires you to say things that may be hard for others to hear. But even words that challenge others can be said with love. When the words you say are in the best interest of those around you, not said to make yourself look bigger or better, they are like a verbal embrace. They support those around you with tender strength.

AN HONEST ANSWER IS LIKE A WARM HUG.
PROVERBS 24:26 MSG

14.
His secrets are safe with you.

God's Spirit continually whispers to the hearts of those in whom He makes His home. He whispers the truth about who you are, how important you are to Him, and His purpose for you in this world. Sometimes His whispers seem inaudible. Their truth may be blocked from you by the distracting busyness of life, inattentiveness, or rebellion. Sometimes God may dim His whisper to encourage you to follow Him whether you are aware of His presence or not. No matter how audible God's whisper is in your life, take time to listen. God has secrets He longs to share with you.

Sharing a secret with a friend is a sacred trust. Imagine God cupping His hand to your ear, whispering words He intends for only you to hear. Feel the sense of intimacy, privacy, and privilege. Then openly share your deepest secrets with Him.

FRIENDSHIP WITH GOD IS RESERVED FOR THOSE WHO REVERENCE HIM. WITH THEM ALONE HE SHARES THE SECRETS OF HIS PROMISES.
PSALM 25:14 TLB

15.
You are fighting a battle against an enemy you can't see.

Invisible armies. Those words sound like the grist of science fiction. After all, you're simply sitting here reading a book, maybe even enjoying a cup of coffee. But God says you are at war. You have an enemy that wants you to turn away from your Heavenly Father, to hightail it and run back to a life that's centered solely on yourself and your own personal pursuit of happiness.

While this battle may wear you down at times—as the enemy reveals himself through relational conflict, circumstantial frustration, or emotional upheaval—there is good news. The war has already been won. Jesus secured the victory the moment He defeated the enemy by rising from the dead.

Though your enemy is fighting a losing battle, he's still fighting. That's why God has made some powerful weapons available to you. In the last chapter of the book of Ephesians, God lists your battle gear: truth, righteousness, God's gospel of peace, faith, the Bible, and the assurance of your salvation.

When trouble comes your way, make sure you're fully dressed for the occasion. Just remember that you're not an army of one. God's power and protection are within prayer's reach. Call for reinforcements.

Never forget that the battle is real and the stakes are high. Though ultimate victory is certain, and your salvation is secure, minor skirmishes can still result in casualties. Consequences such as broken relationships, discouragement, a loss of effectiveness, or a bitter, unforgiving spirit can all result from refusing to step up to the front lines and fight.

Just make sure you're fighting the real enemy. Your battle is not with "flesh and blood," no matter how much your true adversary would like you to believe it is. When a stranger cheats you, a neighbor slights you, or a friend betrays you, recognize that there is more going on than meets the human eye. Go ahead and confront those who've wronged you, but do so with love, forgiveness, and the aim of reconciliation. Don't let relational differences distract you from the bigger battle that is going on for your heart and soul.

The more aware you become that this battle is real, the better you'll be able to fight it—and to recognize the true enemy. This doesn't mean you should spend your life looking for demons behind every hydrangea bush. Not every offhanded remark from a friend, flat tire, or company layoff is a personal spiritual attack. Sometimes, you may simply be reaping the consequences of your own poor choices or the fact that you live in a world tainted by sin.

Be alert, be levelheaded, and call on God for the ability to discern what is going on in situations that come up. Remember that He is there and that "greater is He who is in you than he who is in the world" (1 John 4:4 NASB). You are not alone, and you are not outnumbered.

So don your armor daily, asking God for wisdom and strength. Then move forward with courage and confidence, ready to face whatever comes your way.

WE ARE NOT FIGHTING A BATTLE AGAINST PEOPLE MADE OF FLESH AND BLOOD, BUT AGAINST THE EVIL RULERS AND AUTHORITIES OF THE UNSEEN WORLD.
EPHESIANS 6:12 NLT

16.
Your life bears fruit that won't spoil.

You'll accomplish a lot in your lifetime. You'll work, make friends. You may marry, raise kids, and build a home. You may learn Cantonese or even make the cover of a famous newsmagazine. All of these are wonderful. However, they are not lasting.

The only thing that is eternal, besides God himself, is God's Church, which includes every individual who calls Jesus, Lord. These people are the only "fruit that will last," the eternal apples of God's eye.

Your life here on earth can make this kind of fruit fit for Heaven. Every time you help draw someone closer to God, you are planting seeds that may blossom into lasting fruit.

Scatter the seeds of love, generosity, honesty, and prayer into the lives of those around you. When you get to Heaven, perhaps God will take you on a tour of the living orchard you grew with His help.

JESUS SAID, "I CHOSE YOU. AND I GAVE YOU
THIS WORK: TO GO AND PRODUCE FRUIT,
FRUIT THAT WILL LAST."
JOHN 15:16 NCV

17.
You need spiritual exercise.

In the good old days, people used to work in the fields, walk or ride a horse into town, chop wood, haul water, and knead bread without the help of a fancy electric mixer or bread machine. They didn't need to schedule time for a workout. Life was a workout.

Today, chances are you probably spend much of your day sitting in front of a computer, behind a steering wheel, or in front of the TV. But, God designed your body to move. The more inactive you become, the less efficient your body will be.

What's true for you physically is also true for you spiritually. If you are a spiritual couch potato who knows about God but isn't putting what you know into practice, you're going to become flabby and ineffective. When a God-given opportunity knocks, you may not even be able to jump up and answer the door.

But twenty-four hours a day you have a Personal Trainer who is just a prayer away. Ask God to show you where you are weak spiritually. Then, make a commitment to start working out—today. You can start off slowly, reading only a verse or two each day from the Bible. Choose a translation that is easy for you to understand. A study Bible will also give you additional insight into what you're reading by helping put it into context.

Start with the story of Jesus' life, found in the Gospels. Work your way through Psalms, Proverbs, and the remaining books of the New Testament. Then, tackle the books of history and prophecy found in the Old Testament. You'll be surprised to find how much the lives of people who lived thousands of years ago can teach you about following God in the 21st century.

Next spend a few minutes in prayer. Ask God to help you answer a few questions: What does this teach me about God? What does this teach me about how God feels about me? Is there anything in this passage I need to apply to my life? Spend a few more moments just talking to God, thanking Him for the ways you see Him working in your life, and sharing any concerns you have about your own life and the lives of others.

Don't be deceived into believing that if you've made it this far, you've completed your workout. You're only warming up. The real exercise comes from acting on what God has revealed to you.

In the same way that you build muscle and endurance at the gym, this daily exercise program will strengthen you spiritually. Soon you'll find yourself ready to handle a bit more. Read and study larger portions of the Bible. Set aside a whole afternoon every so often just to talk to God, writing down what you learn so it can help you "exercise" afterwards. Share with others what God is showing you. Join a Bible study group. Memorize Bible verses you find particularly helpful in your daily life. Love others deeply and unconditionally. With God's help, face your worst habits, and most secret sins, head-on. Then, spend time rejoicing in God's unchanging love for you and His power to transform you from a 97-pound weakling into a spiritual bodybuilder extraordinaire.

SPEND YOUR TIME AND ENERGY IN TRAINING YOURSELF FOR SPIRITUAL FITNESS. PHYSICAL EXERCISE HAS SOME VALUE, BUT SPIRITUAL EXERCISE IS MUCH MORE IMPORTANT, FOR IT PROMISES A REWARD IN BOTH THIS LIFE AND THE NEXT.
1 TIMOTHY 4:7–8 NLT

18.
You are unique.

When God formed you in your mother's womb, He fashioned you in a unique way, both inside and out. Even if you were born an identical twin, God's design for you and your life will never be duplicated. You are one of a kind. Rare. Distinctive. And wholly irreplaceable. Without the story of your life, God's own eternal book would be missing a cherished chapter.

If you find yourself feeling lost in a sea of faces, if you feel your accomplishments are insignificant in comparison with those around you, if you feel over-looked or under-loved, remember . . . God created you as an original. No one else throughout the history of time, both past and future, can bring to this world the unique combination of gifts, personality, experience, and love that you can. There's no one else God can use to fill the place He's saved especially for you.

EACH OF US IS AN ORIGINAL.
GALATIANS 5:26 MSG

19.
You can transform worries into prayers.

Everyone has concerns. They have been a normal part of life since the dawn of time. Moses was concerned that Pharaoh wouldn't believe he'd been sent by God to free the Israelites. Solomon was concerned about leading a kingdom wisely. Mary was concerned about having a baby born in a miraculous way. Jesus was concerned about facing death on the Cross.

These concerns may appear to be a step beyond "normal" life. They seem bigger than common concerns, such as keeping your job, losing ten pounds, or finding an honest auto mechanic to service your car. But all concerns, both big and small, need to be approached from the same perspective—God's.

Moses, Solomon, Mary, and Jesus all handled their concerns in the same way. They expressed their concerns in prayer. Once in God's presence, they were reminded of God's love, His power, and His eternal plan. This gave them the strength to move forward and face whatever lay ahead, whether God changed their circumstances or not.

The same opportunity is available to you. You can keep worry from weighing down your life by lifting every one of your concerns straight up to Heaven—the minute they threaten your mind and heart. The sooner you do this, the less time an understandable concern has to transform into a stifling, binding burden of worry.

What concerns do you have today? Have any of them metastasized into worry? Talk to God about it—what you're worried will happen, or won't happen, and why. Prayer invites God to work at the heart of your concern. Best of all, it also invites Him to work in your own heart, guiding you toward both peace and praise, regardless of the "what ifs" that may be whispering to you menacingly from the shadows of possibility.

LET PETITIONS AND PRAISES SHAPE YOUR WORRIES INTO PRAYERS, LETTING GOD KNOW YOUR CONCERNS.
PHILIPPIANS 4:6 MSG

20.
When you suffer, the whole Church suffers.

Your body is made up of an amazing number of interdependent parts: lungs, legs, blood cells, fingernails, and hair follicles, to name only a few. If you had to list the parts of your body from the most important to the least, chances are your appendix wouldn't rank high on the list.

God placed this narrow, three-to-four inch, worm-shaped tube in the lower right part of your abdomen. What does it do? Well, according to doctors, not much. However, if this seemingly insignificant part of the body becomes infected, your whole body can cease to function. In other words, you can die. Suddenly that insignificant part of the body seems to possess an awful lot of power.

In contrast to the ongoing chicken nugget debate, which claims that "parts is parts," parts of the body are not interchangeable. They are each designed for a unique job. If your appendix ruptures, you can't convince your leg to hold things together. If your heart malfunctions, your liver won't be an adequate understudy. In addition, if one part of your body aches, your whole body will be aware of the pain.

The same thing is true for the body of Christ.

The body of Christ, also called the Church, is made up of every individual who chooses to follow God. These individuals make up a seemingly endless variety of parts. God designed some parts to teach, some to serve, some to provide encouragement, and others to pray. Some may care for the babies in the nursery or feed the homeless downtown. Some may travel to distant countries to share God's Good News, while others may stay in the same town where they were born and financially support those half a world away.

In God's plan, every "part" has a special job that no other part could ever fill in exactly the same way. Some parts may seem to be more important than others. The speaker who preaches to tens of thousands of people may seem more vital than the teen who helps quiet babies in the nursery. But the truth is that if one small part, say the "appendix" of the Church, stops functioning, it affects the whole body.

Whatever part of the body God has determined you to be, whatever unique place He has for you to use your talents, you matter. At times you may feel like an often-ignored appendix. You may even question how important your contribution really is. But what you feel does not always give you an accurate picture of what is true.

Remember this when things are going well, and especially when they are not. When you are suffering—physically, emotionally, financially, relationally, or spiritually—the whole body of Christ aches. Along with turning to God for help, don't forget to turn to the body of Christ that you are an integral part of. Share your needs and concerns. Ask friends to pray with you. Accept help when it's offered. Then, when you are fully functioning again, reach out in the same way to others, using your own unique blend of gifts, talents, and experience.

IF ONE PART OF THE BODY SUFFERS, ALL THE OTHER PARTS SUFFER WITH IT. OR IF ONE PART OF OUR BODY IS HONORED, ALL THE OTHER PARTS SHARE ITS HONOR. TOGETHER YOU ARE THE BODY OF CHRIST, AND EACH ONE OF YOU IS A PART OF THAT BODY.
1 CORINTHIANS 12:26–27 NCV

21.
Every circumstance in your life will be used for good.

You've heard the expression, "Into every life a little rain must fall." Sometimes you get a sprinkle. Sometimes you feel like a direct descendent of Noah. Your car breaks down. You lose your job. Your husband has a midlife crisis and leaves you for someone else. Your wife is diagnosed with an incurable disease.

No one would look at these circumstances and declare them "good." Not even God. But God can bring good things out of them. He promises to take everything that happens in your life, both good and bad, and use these experiences to fashion something beautiful.

It's easy to praise God for the days you wish you could relive again and again. But God also wants to play a part in your deepest hurts and darkest moments. Be honest with Him. Include Him in everything from your minor disappointments to your major bouts with despair. You can tell Him how angry you are—even if it happens to be at Him. You can cry and say nothing at all. The Bible says, "The Holy Spirit helps us in our distress. For we don't even know what we should pray for, nor how we should pray. But the

Holy Spirit prays for us with groanings that cannot be expressed in words." (Romans 8:26 NLT)

Keep your eyes and heart open. You may have the opportunity to witness firsthand how God takes tragedy and evil and brings about "good things" such as healing, growth, and change. Chances are, you'll have to wait until Heaven to get the full picture of the good God will bring about through the hard times you went through here on earth. But whether you get a glimmer of understanding in this life, or merely the comfort of hope in what you can't yet see, hold on to the truth that no circumstance is beyond God's power to transform into something worth praising Him for.

WE KNOW THAT IN ALL THINGS GOD WORKS FOR THE GOOD OF THOSE WHO LOVE HIM, WHO HAVE BEEN CALLED ACCORDING TO HIS PURPOSE.
ROMANS 8:28 NIV

22.
You are rich.

How do you measure wealth? By the size of your investment portfolio? The square footage of your home? The make of your car? The amount of money you have at the end of the month? The bottom line of your net worth?

If you use measures such as these to compare yourself to the celebrities you see on TV, or perhaps even the family who lives right next door, you may not consider yourself wealthy. You may even struggle to refer to yourself as "middle class."

But riches you can hold in your hands never last. Fortunes change. The market falls. A medical emergency drains your savings account. The economy goes into a slump. Natural disasters destroy everything you feel you've spent your life trying to build. You die and leave every cent you have to someone else. In light of all this, the good news is that riches that can disappear were never true riches to begin with.

God says you're rich in this life, as well as the next—with riches that can never fade away. You are loved beyond measure. You have been entrusted with priceless gifts and talents. You are an irreplaceable part of God's family. You have God's Spirit living inside you. You have the opportunity to make a positive impact on the people around you. You are the beneficiary of God's grace, forgiveness, hope, peace, power, and joy. All of these things, and many more, are treasures whose worth can be gauged only as "priceless."

Take a moment to consider the riches you possess right now, ones that will last. Then the next time your checking account is running on empty, you receive a cut in pay, or discontent sneaks into your heart over something you want to have but you know you can't afford, remind yourself of how wealthy you really are.

A DEVOUT LIFE DOES BRING WEALTH, BUT IT'S THE
RICH SIMPLICITY OF BEING YOURSELF BEFORE GOD.
1 TIMOTHY 6:6 MSG

23.
Your prayers don't just fade away after God hears them.

When you speak to a friend, your words become just a memory. Your conversations with God become much more. Every one of your prayers is transformed into sweet incense that fills Heaven with its perfume. Imagine, the more you talk to God, the sweeter Heaven's bouquet!

THEY HELD GOLD BOWLS FILLED WITH INCENSE—THE
PRAYERS OF GOD'S PEOPLE!
REVELATION 5:8 NLT

24.
You're holding the world's sharpest sword in your hands.

A sword can be a powerful weapon and tool. It can defend a city or cut branches to build a shelter. It can fell an enemy or free a friend. The sharper the sword, the more efficient it will be—when placed in the right hands.

The right hands for the two-edged sword of God's Word are the hands of those who long to know, and use, God's truth. This truth will cut through the lies that fill the empty philosophies, pointless pursuits, and distorted desires that have been a part of this world ever since Adam and Eve chose to go their own way, instead of God's.

The more you handle God's Word, the better you will become at wielding it and the stronger the impact and power it will have in your life—and the lives of those around you.

THE WORD OF GOD IS LIVING AND ACTIVE AND
SHARPER THAN ANY TWO-EDGED SWORD.
HEBREWS 4:12 NASB

25.

You can approach the God of the universe without fear.

Before Christ entered the world, meeting with God was a frightening experience. Even Moses, whom God called "friend," was allowed only a quick glimpse of God's back as He passed by. That's all a human heart could handle.

Later, when priests entered the Holy of Holies in the temple, a rope was tied to one of their ankles in case they died in God's presence—and had to be dragged out. No one would risk going in to get them. Only those who were cleansed of their sin, and chosen by God, could get close to the Holiest of the Holy, God himself.

Christ's sacrifice changed everything. When Christ died on the Cross, the curtain that kept the Holy of Holies separate from the rest of the temple was torn in two. Now, approaching God was no longer something to be feared; it was something to be anticipated with joy.

The same is true today. God welcomes you into His presence with outstretched arms. There's no need to fear Him, even if you're ashamed of something you've done. Tell Him about it. Express how sorry you are. Then accept His ready forgiveness. Although God is the most powerful force in the universe, and beyond, you can approach God with confident expectation because of what Christ did on your behalf.

BECAUSE OF CHRIST AND OUR FAITH IN HIM, WE CAN
NOW COME FEARLESSLY INTO GOD'S PRESENCE,
ASSURED OF HIS GLAD WELCOME.
EPHESIANS 3:12 NLT

26.
The better you know God, the better you'll know yourself.

In the sixties, "finding yourself" became a national obsession. People tried to accomplish this worthy endeavor through drugs, meditation, sex, vegetarianism, music, and rebellion against traditional forms of authority and commitment. But the question "Who am I?" could be answered in the sixties in only the same way it is today—by letting the One who created you provide the true answer.

In the same way that an artist is the only one who can explain the real story behind the creation of a masterpiece, God is the only One who can help you understand the story that is being lived out in the masterpiece of you. The better you get to know Him, the more clearly you'll hear His voice. The more you understand His plans and purpose behind all of creation, the more you'll understand how you fit into the grand scheme of things.

IT'S IN CHRIST THAT WE FIND OUT WHO WE
ARE AND WHAT WE ARE LIVING FOR.
EPHESIANS 1:11 MSG

27.
You will judge angels.

What part will God's children play in judging angels? No one knows for sure, except God himself. However, the Bible says that this job will be yours in Heaven. Anyone selected to judge angels must have a keen sense of right and wrong, justice and mercy. God's Spirit provides you with all that and more, today and throughout eternity.

YOU KNOW THAT IN THE FUTURE WE WILL
JUDGE ANGELS, SO SURELY WE CAN JUDGE
THE ORDINARY THINGS OF THIS LIFE.
1 CORINTHIANS 6:3 NCV

28.

You are one of the most important things God ever created.

Light. Water. The Grand Canyon. The blue whale. The circulatory system. The solar system . . . God has created some pretty amazing things. But you top the list—you and every other person God has breathed life into since time began.

God sent His Son to earth to save all people. None of God's creation survived Adam and Eve's banishment from God's perfect garden untouched, but people were the only treasure God deemed worth mobilizing a rescue operation for.

The next time you are awestruck by a sunset, gaze in wonder at the intricacy of a wildflower, or find yourself feeling insignificant as you peer over the ridge of the Grand Canyon, remember that you are more important to God than any of these.

GOD DECIDED TO GIVE US LIFE THROUGH THE WORD
OF TRUTH SO WE MIGHT BE THE MOST IMPORTANT OF
ALL THE THINGS HE MADE.
JAMES 1:18 NCV

29.
A broken heart will do you good.

This may not sound very loving. After all, would you say that you want your children or your best friend to suffer a broken heart? But what if someone you love had done something terribly wrong, something that you knew would break the heart of God. You'd want that person to recognize the impact of what he or she had done. You'd want that person to desire to make things right again, to change his or her destructive ways.

That's exactly what God wants. When you turn away from Him, He longs for your heart to break. He wants you to return to Him not only because He loves you but because He knows that's the best thing for you.

THE SACRIFICE YOU WANT IS A BROKEN SPIRIT.
A BROKEN AND REPENTANT HEART,
O GOD, YOU WILL NOT DESPISE.
PSALM 51:17 NLT

30.
You are a letter from God to the world.

The Bible is not the only love letter God has written to this world. Your life is an ongoing 3–D letter announcing to those around you how intimately God is involved in human life.

You don't even have to speak to spread this message. Your actions write volumes. The more love, humility, sacrifice, courage, and trust in God are evident in your life, the louder God's message of hope will be.

YOUR VERY LIVES ARE A LETTER THAT ANYONE CAN READ JUST BY LOOKING AT YOU. CHRIST HIMSELF WROTE IT—NOT WITH INK, BUT WITH GOD'S LIVING SPIRIT; NOT CHISELED INTO STONE, BUT CARVED INTO HUMAN LIVES.
2 CORINTHIANS 3:2 MSG

31.
God has a new name just for you.

Names have always been important to God. One of the first jobs God gave to Adam was naming each of the animals He'd created. Throughout the Bible, God changes people's names to better fit their changing character. Abram, "a high father," became Abraham, "father of a multitude." Jacob was changed to Israel, "the prince who struggles with God." Simon transformed into Peter, "the rock."

What name has God chosen for you? Though it's fun to ponder this question, you'll have to wait until Heaven to uncover the answer. Whatever your new name will be, it will fit you perfectly, because it's been carefully selected by the One who knows you more intimately than anyone else ever will.

"I WILL GIVE TO EACH A WHITE STONE, AND ON THE
STONE WILL BE ENGRAVED A NEW NAME THAT NO ONE
ELSE KNOWS EXCEPT THE ONE RECEIVING IT."
REVELATION 2:17 TLB

32.
Your work matters.

Tax accountant. Sculptor. Sales clerk. Missionary. Hospital volunteer. Astronaut. Ballet dancer. Donut baker. Taxi driver. President of the United States . . . no matter what your "job" title happens to be, your motivation should remain the same: Work as if God himself were responsible for your review.

After all, God is the One you'll ultimately have to answer to. You can't hide from Him in the company washroom. He's aware of your attitude toward your coworkers and superiors. He sees how accurately you fill in your timecard—or where those extra office supplies wind up. He knows your potential and how much of it you're using at any given time. He also sees the times you go above and beyond your job description, even if no one else ever notices.

And this doesn't include only paid positions. Any task you need to accomplish, no matter how big or small, can be done in a way that honors God. This includes the often-overwhelming job of parenting. No paid position will ever carry as much impact as raising the children God entrusts to your care. At home, just as in the workplace, God cares about your attitude, your patient perseverance, and your commitment toward loving excellence.

People may define you by what you do. How you do what you do is of greater concern to God. Give Him the gift of your best today.

IN ALL THE WORK YOU ARE DOING, WORK THE BEST YOU CAN. WORK AS IF YOU WERE DOING IT FOR THE LORD, NOT FOR PEOPLE.
COLOSSIANS 3:23 NCV

33.
You can provide inner refreshment for your friends.

After God created the world and the vast universe that surrounds it, after He separated light from dark and land from sea, after He fashioned countless plants and animals of incredibly complex and creative design, after He breathed life into the very first human being, God declared that everything He'd made was "good."

Yet God's creation wasn't complete. That's because there was one thing that had the potential to be "not good." That one thing was for the man God had created to be able to face life alone. Adam already had relationship. He knew God in a more intimate way than any of us today can fully understand. But that was not enough. God knew that Adam also needed human companionship.

The same is true for you. It's not good for you to spend your life alone. Not every person marries, yet everyone can develop a circle of friends.

A true friend is more than someone to laugh with. It's someone to cry with. Someone you can turn to for help, someone who'll help you face your greatest fears, biggest questions, and even dumbest mistakes. It's someone who will encourage you to mature into the amazing person God created you to be.

While finding a friend such as this may feel like winning the relational lottery, being this kind of a friend to someone else takes more than luck. It takes intentional love, honesty, and sacrifice. It also takes a commitment to help that person grow.

Eve was certainly not the best "friend" in this regard. By pulling Adam the wrong way—away from God—she not only failed to help him grow, but instead she led him one step closer to death itself. You have that same power in a friend's life. You can be a good influence or a bad influence. You can be someone who draws others closer to God or leads them in the opposite, destructive direction. The decision is up to you.

Choose to be a good friend. Offer loving companionship, God-centered advice, and sacrificial support to others. You'll not only develop close relationships, you'll refresh the hearts and souls of those around you—people whom God dearly loves. As you refresh others with a cool drink of love from the well of friendship, you'll find yourself refreshed, as well.

JUST AS LOTIONS AND FRAGRANCE GIVE SENSUAL
DELIGHT, A SWEET FRIENDSHIP REFRESHES THE SOUL.
PROVERBS 27:9 MSG

34.
God knows exactly how long your life will be.

In your mother's womb, God wove together all the threads that would become you . . . your hair color, your bone structure, the timbre of your voice, and the tendencies of your heart. He determined whether you had the talent to sing at the Met or work with disabled children. He supplied the building blocks of your personality and temperament. He also determined how many days you would live on this earth.

How and when you die is not a haphazard event. It's not an accident, even if an "accident" is determined to be its cause. God knows on what day you'll die. That means you don't need to fear the future. How long you live may be out of your hands, but it certainly isn't out of God's.

However, just knowing God's in control doesn't take all of the "fear" out of the prospect of dying. There's so much that remains unknown. Unlike other major transitions in life, all of which are a little nerve-wracking, death does not come with an instruction manual. When you face transitions such as the first day of school, starting a new job, moving to a distant city, or becoming a parent for the first time, you can rely on the experience of others to help paint a picture of what it's going to be like. This lets you know everything's going to be okay.

When it comes to death, the only person who has died, and then lived to tell the tale, is Jesus. Yet after His resurrection, Jesus didn't spend much time talking about death. Instead, He focused His discussions on life. That in itself should tell us something.

Death is just another transition. It's a doorway that will lead us from one life to the next. Certainly, taking a step into the unknown is bound to be unnerving. But God has planned your transition from the temporal into the eternal with meticulous care. Just as His Spirit was present as you were ushered out of the womb into this world, He will be with you when the time comes for you to leave this world and be welcomed into the next.

YOU SAW ME BEFORE I WAS BORN AND SCHEDULED
EACH DAY OF MY LIFE BEFORE I BEGAN TO BREATH.
EVERY DAY WAS RECORDED IN YOUR BOOK!
PSALM 139:16 TLB

35.
You can know God's thoughts.

Suppose God gave you the ability to read people's minds. Then suppose you met an astrophysicist. Unless you happened to be an astrophysicist, chances are that some of the scientist's thoughts would be over your head.

Children of God have a mind-reading ability of sorts. God's Spirit allows you to learn the way He thinks and how He works. But, as in the case of an astrophysicist, you won't be able to comprehend all the mind of God. In Isaiah 55:9 NIV God declares, "As the heavens are higher than the earth, so are my ways higher than your ways and my thoughts than your thoughts."

However, the closer you get to God, the more you'll come to understand His thoughts and, over time, be transformed by them.

GOD'S SPIRIT IS THE ONLY ONE WHO KNOWS
WHAT IS IN GOD'S MIND. BUT GOD HAS GIVEN US HIS
SPIRIT. THAT'S WHY WE DON'T THINK THE SAME WAY
THAT THE PEOPLE OF THIS WORLD THINK.
THAT'S ALSO WHY WE CAN RECOGNIZE THE BLESSINGS
THAT GOD HAS GIVEN US.
1 CORINTHIANS 2:11–12 CEV

36.
Your weakness can reveal God's power.

If you were to describe Jesus' disciple Peter, "perfect" is probably not one of the words that would automatically spring to your mind. Peter's zeal inspired him to try and walk to Jesus on the water. His doubt made him sink like a lead balloon. Peter's devotion led him to boldly declare he'd never turn away from Jesus. That same evening, Peter denied he even knew the Son of God. Not only once, but three times. In spite of his failings, Jesus named Peter "the rock." Though this "rock" seemed far from steadfast, Peter went on to become one of the Church's most influential and courageous founding fathers.

Peter's weaknesses were as visible as his strengths. Perhaps that's one reason God worked so powerfully through his life. Peter wasn't afraid to make mistakes. He tried to do what was right. Sometimes, he failed. When that happened, he picked himself up, reconciled with Jesus, and continued to move forward.

How do you handle mistakes? Try to cover them up? Give yourself a mental thrashing for being so "stupid"? Refuse to put yourself in any situation where you might make one? Pass the blame on to someone else? Or do you go to God, set things straight, then dust yourself off and continue on the path God has set before you?

Following the latter of these options allows God's power to shine through your weaknesses. In this way, your mistakes become opportunities instead of liabilities. God can use them to teach you—and those around you—valuable lessons, to humble a proud heart, to fortify your faith and courage, or to prove to others that it's God's power, and not your own, that truly is your strength.

This doesn't mean that you should be foolhardy. God doesn't want you to make mistakes. However, when they do happen, just remember that God can use them to reveal more of himself to you and to others.

"MY GRACE IS SUFFICIENT FOR YOU, FOR MY
POWER IS MADE PERFECT IN WEAKNESS."
2 CORINTHIANS 12:9 NIV

37.
You have access to a key that opens priceless treasure.

Imagine uncovering a chest that you know is filled with a bounty of treasure. Its value is immeasurable. Its contents are guaranteed to change your life . . . to make it richer, fuller, and more eternally significant. To top it off, the key to this incomparable treasure is in your hands. What do you do?

The obvious answer is to put the key into the lock and open the chest. Only then can the riches inside that chest make a difference in your life. Only a fool would let the key slip from his or her fingers, then turn and leave a priceless treasure behind, unopened.

The amazing thing is, people do exactly that every day. God has set a precious treasure of wisdom, knowledge, and eternal life in front of you—and every other individual. The key to opening this treasure is accepting that God is God and you are not. That is what it means to "fear" the Lord. It doesn't mean you're afraid of God as much as you are in awe of Him. You see Him for who He really is—the unequaled Ruler of all creation.

If it's been awhile since you've taken a good look at the Almighty God, spend a few moments doing just that. If you need a little help getting started, read a few of the psalms. Reflect on how others have described the majesty, creativity, omniscience, mercy, and love of the all-powerful One who has invited you to call Him Father.

Then gaze at the treasure the Father has graciously set before you. Dip into its riches each day, taking hold of God's priceless gifts with open hands and a grateful heart.

HE WILL BE THE SURE FOUNDATION FOR YOUR TIMES, A RICH STORE OF SALVATION AND WISDOM AND KNOWLEDGE; THE FEAR OF THE LORD IS THE KEY TO THIS TREASURE.
ISAIAH 33:6 NIV

38.
You can sin by doing nothing at all.

Sin begins with choice. It's choosing to go in any direction other than the one in which God is leading you. That includes refusing to budge when God says, "Move ahead."

God may be prompting you to help someone in need, to speak the truth, or to give sacrificially of your time or resources. Turning a blind eye, holding your tongue, or rationalizing away your ability to give may not feel like sin. It may feel as if you're doing nothing at all. But inactivity, procrastination, or apathy in response to God is still a choice—a choice to go your own way instead of His. It may not seem as out-and-out wrong as hurting someone, lying, or stealing, but in reality that's exactly what you're doing.

When it comes to sin, you can't pretend to be Switzerland and plead neutrality. When God says "go," it's time to choose wisely. Get up and get moving.

ANYONE WHO KNOWS THE RIGHT THING
TO DO, BUT DOES NOT DO IT, IS SINNING.
JAMES 4:17 NCV

39.
You are always a winner.

Life in this world often leads people to feel like losers. Comparison, criticism, and competition pit individuals in a race against each other, where the winner's circle is small, saved for an elite, exceptional group.

But when Christ was victorious over death, His love brought you into an eternal winner's circle right along with Him. You are victorious, no matter what the world, or temporary circumstances, may seem to say about you. Hold tightly to that truth—you're a winner, today and throughout eternity.

IN EVERYTHING WE HAVE WON MORE THAN
A VICTORY BECAUSE OF CHRIST WHO LOVES US.
ROMANS 8:37 CEV

40.
God remembers your tears.

How significant is a tear? To God, your tears are so important that He does more than notice them. He counts them and saves them. Every single one.

God knows the depth of your sorrow. He knows the intensity of your pain, both physical and emotional. Although He knows better than anyone that this world and its troubles are only temporary, God chooses to join you in your loneliness, disappointment, and grief. Like a mother who feels her children's pain as if it were her own, God's own heart aches along with yours when you are in pain.

So when you cry, remember that you never weep alone. God is right beside you with comfort and compassion, helping wipe away every tear, including those hidden deep within your heart.

YOU KEEP TRACK OF ALL MY SORROWS. YOU HAVE
COLLECTED ALL MY TEARS IN YOUR BOTTLE.
YOU HAVE RECORDED EACH ONE IN YOUR BOOK.
PSALM 56:8 NLT

41.
Your heart knows the way home.

When God created people, He placed a kind of homing device in their hearts that would lead them back to their true home—back to Heaven with Him. You can hear its steady signal in your conscience, in your innate knowledge of the difference between good and evil. You can feel it when you look up at the stars, or into a microscope, and are forced to confront the mystery of how the complexity of creation could possibly have taken place without the intervention of an almighty hand.

Throughout the history of time, this homing device has led people to believe that death cannot be the end, that there is something beyond our brief stay here on planet earth. Though God has placed this homing device into every human heart, there are those who choose to ignore its God-given signal. They may discount it, but they can't silence it.

So they try to drown out this call to their true home by attempting to create heaven here on earth. Possessions, relationships, wealth, fame, sex, power, adventure . . . the list of false heavens is as varied as individuals themselves. But all of these pleasures are temporary and cannot fully drown out the longings that the magnetism of God's own voice is pulling them to fulfill. Instead of finding themselves satisfied, they wind up disappointed and disillusioned, still longing for more.

What is your response to God's call home? Are you listening with the intensity of a bird dog, ears perked up in expectation? Are you responding to what you hear, following God's lead? Or have you turned up the pleasures of life so loudly that you find yourself just hoping that your luck and health don't head south?

Listen to your heart. Go where God leads. Enjoy the blessings God's given you, but recognize that you're not home yet. The best is yet to come.

HE PUT A LITTLE OF HEAVEN IN OUR HEARTS
SO THAT WE'LL NEVER SETTLE FOR LESS.
2 CORINTHIANS 5:5 MSG

42.
You are God's temple.

The grandeur of the temple that Solomon built for God surpassed anything else built in the ancient world. Completed over 1,000 years before Christ's birth, the temple was constructed over a period of seven years by 183,000 artisans and laborers. Its richly carved walls, beams, and doors were made of wood overlaid with gold and jewels, decorated with images of palm trees, pomegranates, and cherubim.

The gold and silver that Solomon's son, David, gathered to build the temple is estimated to have been worth around two billion dollars. Twenty-three tons of gold were used just to cover the walls of the inner sanctum, the Holy of Holies. It has been said that so much gold was used to decorate the temple that it glittered in the morning sun like the fabled city of El Dorado. Solomon wanted to make sure that God's dwelling place was not only holy, but lavish, befitting the King of the universe.

Today God's Spirit does not reside in a building, but inside those who believe in Him. Your body is His temple, a dwelling place for the Most High. How does this change the way you think about yourself?

As you care for the body God has given you, consider Solomon's temple. Are you using quality materials to keep God's temple in good working order? Are you building strong walls with a healthy diet, adequate rest, and exercise—or are you piecing together a makeshift habitat with the cardboard construction of junk food and unhealthy habits? Are you filling your mind with what would please a King—or what would decorate a frat house? Are you using God's temple to worship God—or to serve yourself?

Ask God to help you better understand how you can make your heart, soul, mind, and body a temple that is worthy of His holy presence. He doesn't ask that you decorate the outside with gold and jewels. All He wants is for you to use what He's given you in a way that honors Him.

DO YOU NOT KNOW THAT YOUR BODY IS A TEMPLE OF
THE HOLY SPIRIT WHO IS IN YOU, WHOM YOU HAVE
FROM GOD, AND THAT YOU ARE NOT YOUR OWN?
FOR YOU HAVE BEEN BOUGHT WITH A PRICE:
THEREFORE GLORIFY GOD IN YOUR BODY.
1 CORINTHIANS 6:19–20 NASB

43.
Every one of your prayers will be answered.

Prayer is a mysterious thing. We talk to someone we can't see, often without saying a word out loud, and then we hope that what we've asked for will come true.

People base this "hope" for answered prayer on different things. Some people think that the longer and harder they pray, or the more people they get to join them in asking God for their specific request, the better chance they have of receiving what they've asked for. Others try making "deals" with God . . . "If You help me pass the bar exam, I promise I'll never skip church on Sunday again!" Still others believe they've earned having their prayers answered because of how conscientious they've tried to be in living their faith. Then there are those who hope that if they get the words just right, by praying "in Jesus' name" or throwing in a few "thees" and "thous," that God's ears will be better attuned to what they have to say.

The truth is that there's only one real "hope" we can rely on which assures us that our prayers will be answered. That hope is God's own promise. God promises that anything we ask in prayer, according to His will, will be answered.

Obviously, there are some prayers that are in direct conflict with God's will, such as requests based on selfishness, hate, or greed. But there are also times when we are unsure of what God's will is in a particular situation. At those times, we should follow Jesus' example. He prayed that God's will would be done "on earth as it is in heaven."

The Lord's Prayer lets us know that God's will is not always fulfilled here on earth. People have free will. They can choose to go against God's perfect plan, which in turn can adversely affect the lives of others. Jesus knew this was true. He also knew that what we wish would happen is not always the best thing to happen. The night before He died, Jesus prayed, "Father, if it is Your will, take this cup away from Me; nevertheless not My will, but Yours, be done" (Luke 22:42, NKJV).

Jesus was asking God to save Him from the horrendous death that lay ahead of Him. But Jesus also asked that God would do what He knew was best, regardless of what Jesus desired at that moment. God answered that prayer.

And God answers your prayers, each and every one. He doesn't ignore a single request. Whatever you ask moves God toward action. Not like a magic genie, who when you rub his "prayer lamp" the right way makes all of your wishes come true, but like a Father, who lovingly helps His child move in the direction that's ultimately best.

So, pray with confidence. Feel free to ask God for the deepest desires of your heart—and to fulfill those desires in whatever way is best in line with His will.

Know that your hope for an answer is firmly placed on the promise of a Father who loves you beyond measure. Then keep your eyes open. Your prayer has unleashed the power of a holy God.

THIS IS THE CONFIDENCE THAT WE HAVE IN HIM, THAT IS IF WE ASK ANYTHING ACCORDING TO HIS WILL, HE HEARS US. AND IF WE KNOW THAT HE HEARS US, WHATEVER WE ASK, WE KNOW THAT WE HAVE THE PETITIONS THAT WE HAVE ASKED OF HIM.
1 JOHN 5:14–15 NKJV

44.
With God's help, a fresh start is yours.

Would you like to edit the book of your life? To delete any regrets? To erase bad choices and mistakes? To redeem tragedies by transforming them into something good? It's true that you can't change the events of the past. But when you allow God to work in your heart, you can change how you view the past. In turn, that can change the whole tone, and overall message, of your life story.

No matter what chapter of life you're currently in, whether it's tragedy, comedy, or something in between, God wants to help you write something beautiful. He gives you a fresh start each morning by presenting you with the opportunity to write a brand-new page of your life. Before you begin, it's good to review with God what you wrote the day before. Is there anything you need to make right? Anyone you need to apologize to or forgive? Any offense you need to take before God's throne?

Allow God's grace to help you rewrite any regrets, mistakes, or hard feelings. Take the pen out of your hands and put it firmly into His. Then, take a fresh look at your story from God's point of view. How has it changed? With those changes in mind, you can turn toward the new page of today with the confidence and conviction you need to write a fresh chapter of faith, hope, and love in action.

GOD REWROTE THE TEXT OF MY LIFE WHEN I OPENED
THE BOOK OF MY HEART TO HIS EYES.
PSALM 18:24 MSG

45.
You are a priest.

Suppose you're getting newly acquainted with someone and that person asks, "So, what do you do?" Have you ever answered, "I'm a priest"? You could. Actually, revealing this amazing truth about yourself could start up some interesting conversations!

In the Old Testament, priests were individuals who had the privilege of "meeting" with God and offering sacrifices to Him. When Christ died on the Cross, this elite class ended—at least in the way they were formerly thought of. Christ's sacrifice opened the door for every person who chooses to follow Him to become a priest.

As a member of God's holy priesthood, you can meet with Him anytime, anywhere, to offer sacrifices of worship, thanksgiving, prayer, and loving actions. No high collar or long black robe is required.

YOU ARE GOD'S HOLY PRIESTS, WHO OFFER THE
SPIRITUAL SACRIFICES THAT PLEASE HIM
BECAUSE OF JESUS CHRIST.
1 PETER 2:5 NLT

46.
Rest is yours.

It's been a long day. Your eyelids feel as though there are weights attached to your lashes. The tension in your back and neck insist you've been toting boulders for fifteen hours instead of crossing off minor errands and work-related projects on your To-Do list. Your body longs to lie prone, still, silent, to sink into an oasis of freshly laundered sheets, complete with an oversized pillow simulating a downy cloud drifting aimlessly on a sultry summer afternoon. The promise of rest feels like paradise found.

Jesus offers the fulfillment of that promise when you need it most. But the rest He provides is more than a good night's sleep. It's relief, and release, from whatever may be weighing down your heart.

The emotional burdens you carry are often the heaviest loads of all. But God did not intend for any of His children to bear them alone. When you reach out in prayer, God reaches back with help, hope, and healing.

God's almighty arms hold both tenderness and strength, so you can rest soundly in His love for you, in His power to do the impossible, and in His exclusive plan for your life.

JESUS SAID, "COME TO ME, ALL OF YOU WHO ARE TIRED
AND HAVE HEAVY LOADS, AND I WILL GIVE YOU REST."
MATTHEW 11:28 NCV

47.
You're becoming more like God every day.

People imitate those they admire. Teens wear the styles of their pop idols. Little kids pick up the speech patterns and mannerisms of older, "cooler" siblings. Toddlers learn to "toddle" by watching their parents walk.

The more you read the Bible and listen to your Heavenly Father, the more you'll learn to walk in His ways. However, it's God's Spirit, not your own efforts, that will make your new "family" resemblance more visible day-by-day. You'll never "become" God, like some people of different faiths profess to believe, but you will become more and more like Him. The more you consistently choose God's way over your own, the more His Spirit can work through you, reflecting God's glory and character to a spiritually seeking world.

AS THE SPIRIT OF THE LORD WORKS WITHIN US,
WE BECOME MORE AND MORE LIKE HIM
AND REFLECT HIS GLORY EVEN MORE.
2 CORINTHIANS 3:18 NLT

48.
God has great plans for you.

Even as a kid, you had an idea of what you wanted to be when you grew up, maybe even whom you hoped to marry. But God has a plan for you, one He had in mind even before you were born. His plan is a great one—but it may appear to be different from yours. What God thinks is "great" is perhaps quite different from what first pops into our minds. That does not make it any less wonderful. It's perfect.

When life gets confusing, when your own plans seem to be disappearing like the morning mist, don't panic. Ask God for the wisdom to know what to do next. Then keep your eyes open as He reveals His plans for your future one day at a time.

"I KNOW THE PLANS I HAVE FOR YOU," DECLARES THE
LORD, "PLANS TO PROSPER YOU AND NOT TO HARM
YOU, PLANS TO GIVE YOU HOPE AND A FUTURE."
JEREMIAH 29:11 NIV

49.
You can live an inside–out life.

How long does it take you to get ready to face the world each morning? You may spend some time grooming, and maybe even squeezing in a bit of exercise.

Now consider how much time you take to get ready to face God each day. Whether you dress up or dress down matters little to God. He looks at your heart. Adding a bit of "internal grooming" time to your morning by asking God to maintain a clean and humble heart in you will keep you presentable inside too.

It will also help you greet the day with eyes that see things from God's point of view. That includes seeing other people's hearts, instead of their physical appearance, style of clothes, race, or age.

So don't just open your eyes when your alarm goes off. Open your heart. Allow God to help you live an inside-out kind of life.

"THE LORD DOES NOT LOOK AT THE THINGS MAN
LOOKS AT. MAN LOOKS AT THE OUTWARD APPEARANCE,
BUT THE LORD LOOKS AT THE HEART."
1 SAMUEL 16:7 NIV

50.
You are worth dying for.

Never let a day go by without recalling this life-changing truth: Jesus loved you so much that He was willing to die so you could spend eternity with Him. Love like that should never be forgotten. It should be celebrated—and wholeheartedly returned.

JESUS SAID, "GOD SO LOVED THE WORLD THAT HE GAVE HIS ONLY BEGOTTEN SON, THAT WHOEVER BELIEVES IN HIM SHOULD NOT PERISH BUT HAVE EVERLASTING LIFE."
JOHN 3:16 NKJV

51.
You have a priceless inheritance waiting for you.

Usually people receive an inheritance when someone else dies. But there is one inheritance you can receive only after you leave this world. It's the inheritance God has set aside for you, a treasure of incalculable worth.

What does that inheritance include? You'll have to wait until Heaven to hear what God's "living" will has reserved in your name. But you can be sure that a child of the King is entitled to unimaginable riches. Whatever these blessings are that are waiting for you, you can be certain that they'll never diminish in value or disappear before you reach your eternal home. They are as secure as your final address.

GOD HAS RESERVED A PRICELESS INHERITANCE
FOR HIS CHILDREN. IT IS KEPT IN HEAVEN FOR YOU,
PURE AND UNDEFILED, BEYOND THE REACH
OF CHANGE AND DECAY.
1 PETER 1:4 NLT

52.
You have your own built-in, full-time, forever Counselor.

Put yourself in the disciples' sandals for just a moment. Imagine what it would have been like to have had Jesus as your teacher, counselor, and friend, to be able to turn to Him any time of day with a question or concern. Now imagine sharing what would be your Last Supper with Jesus and your fellow disciples. Judas has stormed off in a rage. There's talk of denial and death. You're beginning to understand that Jesus is saying good-bye. How would you feel? Confused? Afraid? Abandoned?

At that moment, Jesus chose to comfort His disciples with a promise. He promised that God would send His own Spirit into their lives to be a counselor and comforter who would never leave their side. At Pentecost, Jesus' promise was fulfilled. God's Spirit—a supernatural source of wisdom, courage, and power—entered the lives of every believer.

The promise Jesus made during the Last Supper was not only for the disciples around the table. It was also for you. The fulfillment of that promise is alive in you today. When you chose to follow God, His Spirit took up residence in your life. And nothing can make Him move out.

Like the disciples, you have the privilege of experiencing God's presence firsthand. When you have questions and concerns about life, when you're afraid or confused, God's Spirit is there, ready to offer counsel and comfort.

God's Spirit is not the only form of counsel available to you. The advice of close friends—those who know both you and God well—can be invaluable. At other times, the help of a professional counselor may be exactly what you need to help you conquer deep-seated habits or emotional struggles. But God's Spirit is the only Counselor who is always available, twenty-four hours a day, no appointment necessary, no matter where you are.

Don't hesitate to call on Him for help.

JESUS SAID, "I WILL ASK THE FATHER,
AND HE WILL GIVE YOU ANOTHER COUNSELOR,
WHO WILL NEVER LEAVE YOU."
JOHN 14:16 NLT

53.

You were created to make a positive difference in the world.

Every tool has a specific purpose. Hammers are designed to drive nails. Forks were created to get food into your mouth without using your fingers. A pencil sharpener exists solely to sharpen pencils.

You are much more than a simple tool. You are a beloved child. Yet God also created you to accomplish good things.

In this world, you play an important part. You have the power to make it a better place. At times you may feel like one very small cog in one incredibly oversized wheel, but you fill a spot no one else can fill. From that unique place you have the opportunity to do good works, to be available with the right gifts at the right place at the right time. Without you, who knows what we'd be missing in this world?

WE ARE HIS WORKMANSHIP, CREATED IN CHRIST JESUS FOR GOOD WORKS, WHICH GOD PREPARED BEFORE-HAND THAT WE SHOULD WALK IN THEM.
EPHESIANS 2:10 NKJV

54.
Angels are watching over you right now.

You are never alone. Not only does God never leave your side, He has ordered His angels to care for you. This doesn't mean that you will never get hurt, that you can dive off Niagara Falls even without a barrel and be assured you'll survive. What it does mean is that God and His angels are involved in your daily life. Nothing happens to you that God is unaware of, that He does not allow. His angels are fighting battles on your behalf that you may never be aware of. But they're there. Powerful and ever-present.

HE ORDERS HIS ANGELS TO PROTECT YOU
WHEREVER YOU GO.
PSALM 91:11 NLT

55.
Your words reveal what your heart is like.

What you say exposes who you really are. If you say kind words to someone's face but cruel ones behind the person's back, the true condition of your heart becomes evident—to those around you and, if you're paying attention, to yourself.

If you want to break a habit of gossip, negativity, cursing, exaggeration, or insensitivity, the key isn't holding your tongue. It's cleansing your heart. Ask God to help you honestly face your own pride, rebellion, and selfishness. You'll not only come away with a healthier heart, but with more positive, powerful speech.

Jesus said, "It's your heart, not the dictionary,
that gives meaning to your words.
A good person produces good deeds and words
season after season."
Matthew 12:34 msg

56.
You have the ability to make money.

When you work, you get something in return. If you shovel snow, you wind up with an ice-free driveway. If you're a mom, that "something" may simply be the joy of knowing you did a good job caring for the children God has entrusted to you. If you work for an employer, you get a paycheck.

The name on your paycheck names the person who did the work. But that doesn't tell the whole story. You didn't accomplish this task on your own. God provided you with the opportunities and abilities necessary to earn the money.

That's cause for praise. Payday should be a time of thanks, not only because you can buy groceries or pay your mortgage, but because God has helped provide for you in a tangible way. Saying "thanks" to Him in prayer is one way of showing your gratitude. Another way is evident in how you choose to spend what you've been given.

Since you recognize that the paycheck comes from God don't forget to give part of the money back to Him. In the Old Testament, people were encouraged to give back to God 10 percent of everything they earned. This is still a good practice for today. Giving to your local church also reminds you that what you've earned isn't wholly yours. God helped you earn it.

Giving away a portion of your monthly income also loosens the grasp that money may have on your heart. This opens the door to a more generous lifestyle. Giving to the church is just the beginning. You are surrounded by a world in need. Perhaps one reason God gave you the ability to do the work you do is so you can provide for others who do not have the same money-making opportunities and abilities as you.

Next paycheck, why not let your generosity sound a loud "thank you" to God? You will bless God, bless your church, bless those in need, and help remove any hold that greed's sticky fingers may have on your heart. That financial investment will pay eternal dividends.

REMEMBER THE LORD YOUR GOD, FOR IT IS HE WHO
GIVES YOU THE ABILITY TO PRODUCE WEALTH.
DEUTERONOMY 8:18 NIV

57.
Even the smallest thing you do for God matters.

You don't have to be a missionary in a third-world country to do something significant for God. If God can use faith the size of a mustard seed to move a mountain, He can certainly use your humble, heartfelt efforts to impact the world in a wonderful way—even if what you do seems small in your own eyes.

No act of love, even those that may seem futile or insignificant, is ever wasted. Suppose you offer a word of encouragement to a young mom who is having an especially difficult day with her kids at the grocery store. Your words could lighten her heart enough to give her an extra dose of patience in dealing with her children the next morning. In turn, her could feel better about himself when he gets to school, where he winds up treating the teacher with more respect than he has lately been in the habit of giving. That teacher could then go home and be better able to handle the demands of her own children. The cycle can go on and on, helping others to become more of the people God desires them to be. And it all started with one little act of love.

Don't hesitate to attempt great things for God. But at the same time, don't miss out on sharing your love in little ways throughout the day. With God's help, a simple act of kindness can end up moving a mountain.

THROW YOURSELVES INTO THE WORK OF THE MASTER, CONFIDENT THAT NOTHING YOU DO FOR HIM IS A WASTE OF TIME OR EFFORT.
1 CORINTHIANS 15:58 MSG

58.
God's law is written on your heart.

You know what God wants you to do—and not do. You may not know the Ten Commandments. You may have never even read the Bible. But you still know. That's because God did not just write His laws on stone tablets to be given to Moses; God wrote His laws on the human heart.

This holy imprint has been made on every individual. Then why isn't the world a more godly place? Because God also gave us the gift of free will. We each get to choose what we'll do with this knowledge.

Listen to your heart. It knows which way God wants you to go. From there, the choice is up to you.

THE LORD SAID, "I WILL WRITE MY LAWS IN THEIR MINDS SO THAT THEY WILL KNOW WHAT I WANT THEM TO DO WITHOUT MY EVEN TELLING THEM, AND THESE LAWS WILL BE IN THEIR HEARTS SO THAT THEY WILL WANT TO OBEY THEM."
HEBREWS 8:10 TLB

59.
Your troubles are temporary.

Some days seem to last forever—especially difficult days that are twisted and torn by pain and trouble. But the truth is that every problem you're experiencing right now will have an end. Keeping that end in sight can help you persevere while you anticipate that time of freedom.

Your problem's resolution may be right around the corner. But it also may not become a reality until you reach the gates of Heaven. That may seem too far away to bring much encouragement right now, but in light of eternity your life is as brief as a single breath.

Instead of putting on proverbial rose-colored glasses to help you see the world and your present problems in a more positive light, try looking at difficulties from God's point of view. Focus on what truly matters. Remember God's goal of helping your love deepen and mature. Keep eternity in mind.

Then, ask God for the strength to face today in light of His promise of tomorrow. Look in His Word for the promises you need to get you through. Hold those close to your heart—memorize them; pray them.

And ask your friends to pray for you or find a believer
you respect and ask them to pray. God never meant
you to face this alone, so don't. And remember that
He is with you, helping you in ways you can't see right
now. Don't ever forget that He loves you right now
with the same love that brought Christ to earth. He
will help you hang on.

OUR LIGHT AND MOMENTARY TROUBLES ARE ACHIEV-
ING FOR US AN ETERNAL GLORY THAT FAR OUTWEIGHS
THEM ALL. SO WE FIX OUR EYES NOT ON WHAT IS SEEN,
BUT ON WHAT IS UNSEEN. FOR WHAT IS SEEN IS TEMPO-
RARY, BUT WHAT IS UNSEEN IS ETERNAL.
2 CORINTHIANS 4:17–18 NIV

60.
Nothing can separate you from God's love.

There are a lot of things that can separate you from those you love. Distance. Work. Conflict. Sickness. Unforgiveness. Time. Misunderstandings. Goals. Circumstances. Death.

Your relationship with God is the only one you'll ever have that cannot be divided. There is no sin evil enough, no conflict grievous enough, no distance far enough, no time long enough, no difference great enough to keep you apart once you've been joined together through Christ's sacrifice.

So rest in the unfathomable depth of God's relationship with you. It's a love nothing can change.

NOTHING IN ALL CREATION CAN SEPARATE US FROM
GOD'S LOVE FOR US IN CHRIST JESUS OUR LORD!
ROMANS 8:39 CEV

61.
You have a spiritual gift.

Before you were born, God chose certain talents and abilities to weave into the unique creation called "you," such as an aptitude for mathematics or a flair for interior design. When you were born a second time—when you asked God to take His rightful place as Lord of your life—God presented you with a brand-new ability called a spiritual gift.

This gift comes to you through the power of God's Spirit, and its purpose is to benefit God's church. Just as He does in the womb, God carefully chooses each special gift to fit its recipient. These gifts include talents such as teaching, encouragement, and praying for others. Every individual may help out in a variety of ways at different times, such as praying for others, but when God places His spiritual gift in you to fill a certain job, you'll find that doing this job comes naturally, brings results, and gives you joy.

Some gifts attract more attention than others. People may find themselves awed by a pastor's ability to communicate deep biblical truths. These same people may give little thought to the person who cleans the sanctuary after the rest of the congregation has headed home for Sunday brunch. But every spiritual gift is vitally important—and significant in God's eyes. If God gave everyone the gift of preaching, who would be left to listen? Who would balance the church budget, sing in the choir, or organize volunteers to reach out to help the surrounding community?

If you are unsure of what gift or gifts God has given you, ask Him for wisdom. Ask those who know you well how they see God working through you in the lives of others. You may even want to see if the leadership of your church has material available that can help you in this area.

Once you have an idea of the nature of the gift God has blessed you with, put that knowledge to use by getting to work. The more you use and develop your gift, the more you'll add to the health of your church—and the contentment of your heart.

A SPIRITUAL GIFT IS GIVEN TO EACH OF US AS A
MEANS OF HELPING THE ENTIRE CHURCH.
1 CORINTHIANS 12:7 NLT

62.
Perfect peace is available to you.

"Peace on earth" sounds great on a Christmas card, but it's hardly a reality. At least, that's the way it looks if you read the morning paper. But remember, there's more to life than what you can see with your eyes.

When Jesus was born, the angels proclaimed, "Glory to God in the heavenly heights, peace to all men and women on earth who please him" (Luke 2:14 MSG). Peace on earth is made a reality with God. And that reality is visible only to the world through the lives of those who keep close to God's side.

God's Spirit, and His peace, are just as real as your circumstances. Turning to God frequently throughout the day—asking for His guidance, comfort, and perspective—will help you see beyond your circumstances. It will help you refocus on the Author of life itself.

Even when your outward life is in total chaos, God offers you a place of retreat and restoration. And the more often you choose to visit, the easier it will be for you to experience God's peace in a real and profound way. Call on Him anytime you need a little patch of "peace on earth." He never tires of hearing your voice.

HE WILL KEEP IN PERFECT PEACE ALL THOSE WHO TRUST IN HIM, WHOSE THOUGHTS TURN OFTEN TO THE LORD!
ISAIAH 26:3 TLB

63.
Everything God has belongs to you.

Picture yourself as a slave. You have few, if any, rights. Your master makes the rules and can change them at any time, according to his mood or whim. When your master dies, you have no right to anything he owned. After all, you yourself are really only a possession. You can be given away or passed down to someone else as easily as the family china.

Now picture yourself as a child. Cherished. Nurtured. Perhaps even pampered. Not a possession, but a person. Part of a family whose ties extend forward and backward through generations. In most cases, when your parents die, what they own will be passed on to you. It will legally become yours.

At one time, you were a slave to sin. You had a master who truly was your enemy. He didn't care about you. He simply wanted to rule over you. To take all you had for his very own.

Once you became part of God's family, your ties with that cruel master were severed. Oh, he may come around every now and then trying to convince you that he's still in charge. But the truth is, you've been adopted into a new family. You have traded a relationship with a deceitful slave owner for that of a loving

Father. Now you truly are cherished, nurtured, and deeply loved.

What's more, you have received the rights that befit a beloved child. You share in what your Father owns. The cattle on a thousand hills. The sun, the moon, and every celestial creation. Priceless riches of the heart. Eternal life . . .

You are a privileged child. Why not take a moment right now and thank your Father for who He is, for all He's done, and for all He wants to share with you through time without end.

YOU ARE NO LONGER A SLAVE BUT GOD'S
OWN CHILD. AND SINCE YOU ARE HIS CHILD,
EVERYTHING HE HAS BELONGS TO YOU.
GALATIANS 4:7 NLT

64.
You're at your greatest when you serve.

God's kingdom seems a little topsy-turvy when compared with the world. The rich are regarded as poor in heart, while the poor are considered to be rich in what matters most. Those who are willing to admit their weaknesses become those who are ultimately the strongest through God's power. And the people who humble themselves to serve others, often going unnoticed by the world, are those who are most honored by God.

Refuse to judge yourself or your life by the praise, criticism, or even indifference of the world. The world's way is not God's way. Serve others with your whole heart, striving more to extend love than to be noticed. That's how you'll truly make it to the top.

JESUS SAID, "THE MORE LOWLY YOUR SERVICE TO
OTHERS, THE GREATER YOU ARE. TO BE
THE GREATEST, BE A SERVANT."
MATTHEW 23:11 TLB

65.
God knows what you do in secret.

"He sees you when you're sleeping. He knows when you're awake. He knows if you've been bad or good, so be good for goodness sake . . ." If you review the "facts," Santa Claus really doesn't seem like all that great a guy. Okay, so he's generous. But only with those who he decides have earned his good gifts. He affords you no privacy, takes notes on everything you do, and makes the ultimate judgment of which list you're going to be on—the good list or the bad one. He decides whether you get a new trike or a lump of coal by seeing if the good you've done outweighs the bad.

Some people base their image of God on the myth of Santa. They picture their Heavenly Father wearing a judgmental scowl and wielding a giant red pen, just waiting to record some secret sin.

It's true that God does see us when we're sleeping and knows when we're awake. He sees everything we do, both good and bad. More than that, He's aware of everything we think, every hate-filled opinion or cuss word concealed behind smiling, closed lips. And every time He sees something akin to what Santa would record on his "bad" list, God's heart breaks.

Unlike the mythical figure of Santa, God is not an uninvolved bystander. God loves every person He sees. He rejoices when His children choose good and grieves when they choose evil. But when God's children go the wrong way, He doesn't automatically dole out that lump of coal. Because of what Jesus did on the Cross, God offers forgiveness instead.

Yes, God knows what you've done—every praise-worthy, cruel, or worthless thought and action. But that isn't cause to fear Him. It's reason to turn to Him. To confess where you've blown it. To ask for forgiveness. To bask in the joy of a judgment of "not guilty" when you finally meet Him face-to-face.

THE DAY WILL SURELY COME WHEN GOD, BY JESUS
CHRIST, WILL JUDGE EVERYONE'S SECRET LIFE.
ROMANS 2:16 NLT

66.
You can help fight others' battles.

Your prayers, your love, your time, and your resources can all play a vital part in the victory of those around you. They can be a life preserver when troubles threaten to overwhelm them or a sword when they are up against an enemy that may not even be visible to the human eye.

Where, and how, does God want you to get involved in fighting others' battles? The only way to find out is to ask Him. Just be ready and willing to act when He moves your heart in compassion toward joining in another's fight. God may use you as part of the cavalry that shows up at just the right time—and changes the final outcome of the war.

YOU AND YOUR PRAYERS ARE PART
OF THE RESCUE OPERATION.
2 CORINTHIANS 1:10 MSG

67.
You will be fully satisfied only when you are with God.

Like an itch you can't reach or the hunger for fresh strawberries when they're no longer in season, this life will always leave you wanting. Even when you've found true contentment in the life God has allowed you to live, there will always be a dull longing for something more, something that fully satisfies. That longing can be quenched only by something that's available after death—a face-to-face encounter with your true soul mate, God himself.

WHEN I AWAKE IN HEAVEN, I WILL BE FULLY SATISFIED,
FOR I WILL SEE YOU FACE TO FACE.
PSALM 17:15 TLB

68.
Your life is being refined.

Refining is a process of purification. It removes the impurities that taint a precious substance, such as oil, silver, or gold. Intense heat is used to bring impurities to the surface. There they can easily be skimmed off, leaving what is most precious behind—now worth much more than when it was first put over the fire.

Your life is precious to God, so He is putting you through a refining process as well. The good news about finding yourself in hot water, courtesy of God, is that your faults and weaknesses are exposed. As they are brought to the surface, they are easier for you to recognize and, with God's help, deal with. This process is painful, but productive. It's the only way that the true you, and the beauty of your true worth, can shine through for all to see.

"I HAVE REFINED YOU, THOUGH NOT AS SILVER; I HAVE TESTED YOU IN THE FURNACE OF AFFLICTION."
ISAIAH 48:10 NIV

69.
You are free.

Some people regard those who follow God as captives of a set of rules. They claim that only a life where "anything goes" is truly free. But God's Spirit opens our eyes to the truth that being freed by God's love is the only way to experience true freedom.

In the same way that traffic laws prevent the streets from becoming continually chaotic and dangerous, God's laws open the door to living a life that works—one where you are finally free to be yourself and safely reach your final destination.

You still have free will, whether you choose to follow God or not. In that way, "anything" does still go. However, using your free will to make wise choices—to act on what you learn in the Bible—will lead you to the liberty of a life guided by love, empowered by faith, and bathed in grace.

THE LORD IS THE SPIRIT, AND WHERE THE SPIRIT OF
THE LORD IS, THERE IS FREEDOM.
2 CORINTHIANS 3:17 NCV

70.

You are a work in progress that will be completed.

God will never leave incomplete what He has begun in you. He will never abandon His plan or abort His purpose in your life. You will never die before God's had a chance to finish what He's started in you. As long as you place your trust in God and follow Him, God will continue to complete the good work He is doing in you, working productively right up until His finished product is unveiled in Heaven—you as you were created to be.

I AM SURE THAT GOD, WHO BEGAN THE GOOD
WORK WITHIN YOU, WILL CONTINUE HIS WORK
UNTIL IT IS FINALLY FINISHED ON THAT DAY
WHEN CHRIST JESUS COMES BACK AGAIN.
PHILIPPIANS 1:6 NLT

71.
Your body is just a temporary tent.

Picture yourself on a campout. The winds have been howling ever since you arrived. However, the recent onset of nightfall seems to have stirred the air currents into a frenzy, threatening near hurricane status. As the first raindrops—the size of hamsters—begin to fall, water quickly seeps through the seams of your tent. Foregoing any hope of sleep, you count the individual drops and name the river—that begins to form beneath your sleeping bag—after yourself. As the temperature continues to fall, the rain turns quickly into snow. Lying on the rock-hard and soon-to-be-frozen ground, while trying to fend off hypothermia, the only thing that is going through your mind at a time like this is, "I want to go home!"

Sometimes life feels like a bad camping trip, with your body serving as that poor, windblown tent. Yes, your body is God's temple. But it's only a temporary one. It's like the tabernacle that the Israelites carried around in the desert for forty years. It adequately served its purpose as a dwelling place for the Most High while the Israelites were on the move. But once they made it home to the Promised Land, it was time to leave that portable tent behind and build something more permanent and beautiful, befitting their one, true King.

One day you'll have the chance to enter the eternal Promised Land. At that time, you'll receive a new and improved permanent body along with your permanent address. A body that won't break down or give out as time goes by. A dwelling that will last forever. But until that day comes, there may be days when dwelling in this flimsy tent of the human body may prove more than just uncomfortable. It may be downright painful.

When physical problems threaten to dim God's gift of joy in your life, when pain is unrelenting or healing seems out of reach, reach out to God. The Great Physician may not choose to provide instant relief. He may allow your physical tent to flap violently through the natural storms of life. But with the comfort of God's love, you can relax in the eye of the storm. God's presence can provide a place of peace and growth, even when you find yourself in the most inhospitable of surroundings. And when the right time comes, God will help you take down one last time the temporary tent He's given you and leave it behind on the trail as you make your way home.

WE KNOW THAT WHEN THIS TENT WE LIVE IN IS TAKEN DOWN—WHEN WE DIE AND LEAVE THESE BODIES—WE WILL HAVE WONDERFUL NEW BODIES IN HEAVEN, HOMES THAT WILL BE OURS FOREVERMORE, MADE FOR US BY GOD HIMSELF.

2 CORINTHIANS 5:1 TLB

72.
You have a built-in desire to worship God.

It isn't only an appreciation of beauty that inspires a sense of awe when you watch a thunderous procession of ocean waves or witness the transient, vibrant hues of an autumn sunset. It's your innate desire to worship God.

The blessings and beauty we encounter in life, the times we find ourselves overwhelmed with the knowledge that we seem so small in the midst of an intricately organized universe, the moments when we recognize that we are not in control—but Someone else is—are all invitations to visit the throne of the almighty God . . . to bow down in wonder, gratitude, and humility . . . to worship in prayer, in song, in silence, and in acts of love.

THIS IS WHAT THE LORD, THE GOD OF ISRAEL, SAYS: "I WILL PUT A DESIRE IN THEIR HEARTS TO WORSHIP ME."
JEREMIAH 32:40 NLT

73.
You were made for love.

Bicycles were invented to get people from one place to another. Mittens were designed to keep hands warm despite the winter's chill. Stoplights were created to help the flow of traffic move more smoothly. People were made for love.

God created mankind out of His longing for relationship. That is why the blueprint for human design reflects a single purpose—to give and receive love. God created human beings to lavish His love on so they could, in turn, love each other and Him.

Live within your blueprint. Fulfill your perfect purpose. Love God and love people with everything you have.

GO AFTER A LIFE OF LOVE AS IF
YOUR LIFE DEPENDED ON IT—BECAUSE IT DOES.
1 CORINTHIANS 14:1 MSG

74.
You can find more satisfaction in God than in a hot fudge sundae.

Imagine being seated before a never-ending dessert buffet. All of your favorites lay before you . . . caramel-topped cheesecake, warm chocolate chip cookies, fresh peach pie, homemade apple strudel, a mountain of snickerdoodles, a sea of chocolate truffles, and the makings of a hot fudge sundae you could take up residence in. Even the most discerning palate would be sure to find something that would satisfy the sweet tooth that lurked within.

It sounds like a dream come true. But what happens after your attempt to satisfy yourself gets out of hand, when your pants start to feel tight and your stomach starts to ache? And what about the day after, when the momentary satisfaction you received from a mouthful of fudge the previous afternoon has left you with nothing more to show than a few extra pounds?

Delicious food tempts you with the promise of satisfaction, but it's a promise food can't fully live up to. Neither can a new car, a bigger house, a more exotic vacation, or a different spouse. The only thing that can truly satisfy your inner hunger, that emptiness within, is the presence of your Heavenly Father.

So the next time you're surveying the pantry,

looking for the perfect snack to satisfy a serious case of the munchies, or perusing the sale rack of your favorite boutique in search of something to lift your spirits, take a moment to ask yourself, *What am I really hungry for?* You may find that your restless longing is really a desire for something this world can never offer—the peace of mind and heart that comes only from closely following God.

YOU SATISFY ME MORE THAN THE RICHEST OF FOODS.
PSALM 63:5 NLT

75.
You can talk to God anytime, anywhere, about anything.

Anytime is the right time to talk to God. Stuck in a traffic jam. Picnicing in the park. Arguing with your spouse. Hugging your newborn child. The middle of the night. The break of dawn. All by yourself or lost in a crowd. When you're happy, sad, or anything in between.

God is there. Willing to listen. Ready to act. Call on Him. Today. Tomorrow. Always.

You'll never have to ask, "Can You hear me now?" To Him, your voice will always be crystal clear.

PRAY IN THE SPIRIT AT ALL TIMES WITH ALL KINDS OF
PRAYER, ASKING FOR EVERYTHING YOU NEED.
EPHESIANS 6:18 NCV

76.
You can't earn the gift of eternal life.

When the day finally arrives when you find yourself at home in Heaven, you'll also find you're going to share this eternal paradise with lots of unsavory characters . . . murderers, liars, adulterers, and thieves. And that's just for starters.

The thought of your future neighbors may make you a little uneasy. You may even find yourself praying that their eternal mansions are located on the other side of the proverbial tracks. After all, chances are you've led a pretty decent life. Sure, you may have lied here and there, but almost all of these could be considered little white lies, right? And other than the occasional parking ticket, you've probably never been on the run from the law. That should count for something, shouldn't it?

Doing the right thing makes God smile. And that counts for a lot. It gives God pleasure to watch His children grow close to Him and learn to love others well. Making godly choices also makes your own life easier and allows you to effect a more positive impact on the world around you. But one thing that doing what is right does not do is get you into Heaven. Only Christ's death on the Cross has the power to do that.

That's because God is 100 percent holy. No fillers. Nothing artificial. Not one iota of evil. God can't stand even being in the company of anything evil. And all of us have cultivated pockets of evil in our lives. Some people's pockets may hold a bit more than others. But evil is evil. A big sin and a small sin are at their core exactly the same thing—rebellion against God.

In the Old Testament, God appointed priests who performed sacrifices which cleansed people of their recently committed sins. Somehow through this process, a holy God was once again able to be in the presence of an often unholy people. But the problem was that the priests had to perform these sacrifices over and over again because people continued to turn from God over and over again.

Although God gave the world the Ten Commandments, not one person could fully live up to them. Even righteous people such as Moses and David blew it now and then, sometimes in very big ways. But God would not give up on mankind. His love was too deep. That's why He sent His Son.

Jesus became the once-and-for-all sacrifice. His death on the Cross paid for every sin committed from the creation of the world until its inevitable end. Every punishment we deserve to receive for sins, big and small, Jesus took upon himself. It was this unselfish act, this perfect gift of grace, that gives us the opportunity to spend eternity in God's holy presence.

But this opportunity is one we have to reach out and accept. By acknowledging what Christ did for us, by admitting our own sin and humbly receiving God's

gracious free gift, we heal our relationship with God—
and receive our permanent place in Heaven as part of
His family.

In Heaven we will be with people whose mortal
lives may have differed widely from our own. From
our present earthly perspective, we may feel as though
we may be more worthy—or perhaps less—than some
of our future neighbors. But once we enter Heaven
and finally see things from God's perfect perspective,
we will be able to fully recognize ourselves and others
for what we truly are—one family, one body, one
Church, all wholly loved and fully forgiven, equally
undeserving recipients of the priceless gift of God's
amazing grace.

BY GRACE YOU HAVE BEEN SAVED THROUGH FAITH;
AND THAT NOT OF YOURSELVES, IT IS THE GIFT
OF GOD; NOT AS A RESULT OF WORKS,
SO THAT NO ONE MAY BOAST.
EPHESIANS 2:8–9 NASB

77.
You were patterned after God.

Every snowflake is one of a kind, unique in its own individually intricate frosty design. But at the same time, all snowflakes are made from the same basic pattern of interlocking ice crystals. When you melt them down to their fundamental components, they become uniform in appearance. They all look like one very tiny puddle.

In the same way, there is only one you. Not only does your physical and emotional makeup differ from the rest of humanity, but so do your personal history, your distinctive blend of gifts and talents, and the way you relate to others, including God.

But there is also something you have in common with the rest of mankind. Your basic design was patterned in the image of God. That doesn't mean that people were created as mini-gods, cookie-cutter reflections of the Almighty. What it does mean is that there's a family resemblance between you and your Heavenly Father. What the extent of this is will become clear only when we meet God face-to-face.

However, the fact remains that when people look at you they also get a glimpse of God, a peek at His image. The same thing is true when you look at them.

Look for God in the faces of those around you today. Remember that each one of them—and that includes the one you see reflected in the mirror—is His beloved child, someone made in His miraculous image.

GOD CREATED PEOPLE IN HIS OWN IMAGE; GOD
PATTERNED THEM AFTER HIMSELF.
GENESIS 1:27 NLT

78.
You can deceive yourself, but not God.

You may feel you know yourself pretty well. Better than anyone else does, at least. But God knows you even better than you know yourself. That's because God not only created your heart, but He can see into its darkest corners. He knows the mixed motives, secret desires, and buried resentments that may be hiding there, unknown to even you.

That's why we all need God as our compass as we travel through life. The human heart can lead us in the wrong direction. It can deceive us into thinking wrong is right. But God never will.

GIVE YOUR PEOPLE WHATEVER THEY DESERVE,
FOR YOU ALONE KNOW THE HUMAN HEART.
2 CHRONICLES 6:30 NLT

79.
You are a source of hope other people need.

The quest for happiness and the meaning of life is a universal pursuit. But pursuing this search on any road other than the one that leads straight to Jesus is a dead end. Literally.

But you already know that. And that knowledge provides you with a rich source of hope. Just like a water tanker driver in the middle of the desert, there are people thirsty for that taste of hope. Thirsty for what you have. How willing are you to share it with them?

It's true that discussing the topic of faith can make people feel a bit uncomfortable. That's because people are afraid that their opinions and lifestyle may be opposed or dismissed. While debating theological topics can be helpful to some people, most "hope thirsty" listeners just want to know you are really listening to what they have to say—and that you care about them as individuals.

Sharing your hope begins with reaching out in love, just like Jesus did. Listen carefully when people share with you the things they value most deeply in life. Ask questions. Listen respectfully to their answers, even if you disagree with the conclusions they've reached.

Only then have you really earned the right to share your own story. And that's all you need to do. Talk about how God has made a difference in your life. Be honest. Be real. Don't use religious-sounding words. Just share your heart, your joy, even your questions.

If you don't know the answer to some of the questions thirsty friends ask, tell them you'll try and find out. Then seek out your pastor or someone else you feel is further along the spiritual road than you are. See if they have an answer that may help both you and your friend understand God a bit better.

You never know when a thirsty soul is going to appear on the horizon, headed your way. So keep your eyes and heart open, always ready to hold out a refreshing taste of true hope.

ALWAYS BE PREPARED TO GIVE AN ANSWER TO
EVERYONE WHO ASKS YOU TO GIVE THE REASON FOR
THE HOPE THAT YOU HAVE. BUT DO THIS WITH
GENTLENESS AND RESPECT.
1 PETER 3:15 NIV

80.
You are immortal.

It sounds like something out of a superhero comic strip, but it's true. You are immortal. Nothing can destroy you. The same isn't true of your physical body. But that isn't really who you are anyway. You are so much more. And so much more awaits you than life on this often sorrow-filled earth. You have all of eternity to enjoy growing closer to God and experiencing the true meaning of joy.

THE WORLD AND EVERYTHING THAT PEOPLE WANT IN IT ARE PASSING AWAY, BUT THE PERSON WHO DOES WHAT GOD WANTS LIVES FOREVER.
1 JOHN 2:17 NCV

81.
Hard times are good for you.

You're at the gym. You're working hard. You're sweating. Your muscles are aching. You're watching the clock, counting the minutes until you can head to the showers. But after you've finished, how do you feel? Tired, yet triumphant. You know that what you just went through has done good things for you. Tomorrow you'll be stronger than you were today.

Hard times are like a strenuous workout at the gym—with Attila the Hun serving as your personal trainer. They may stretch you farther than you ever thought you could go, but they do produce some positive results along the way. They force you to turn to God for help, instead of relying solely on your own strength. This supplies your faith and trust in God with what they need to grow.

Patience is a by-product of this personal stretching. The more your patience is developed, the less time you spend in life watching the clock. You find it easier to trust in God's timing, to turn your back on the hollow promise of instant gratification, to allow yourself and others the grace to grow—and make mistakes along the way.

The next time trouble comes your way, call on

God for help. Then put on your workout clothes and get busy. Good things are going to come your way as a result of the tough times ahead.

WE CAN REJOICE, TOO, WHEN WE
RUN INTO PROBLEMS AND TRIALS FOR WE KNOW
THAT THEY ARE GOOD FOR US—THEY HELP US
LEARN TO BE PATIENT. AND PATIENCE DEVELOPS
STRENGTH OF CHARACTER IN US AND HELPS US
TRUST GOD MORE EACH TIME WE USE IT UNTIL FINALLY
OUR HOPE AND FAITH ARE STRONG AND STEADY.
ROMANS 5:3–4 TLB

82.
You are God's hands and feet.

After Jesus rose from the dead and returned to Heaven, God's hands and feet left the soil of this earth. Or so it would seem. But when God guides us to reach out to others in love, to feed the hungry, to comfort the grieving, to provide for the poor, to tend to those who are ill in body or spirit, or to share God's message of hope with those who are searching for the truth, we are acting on God's behalf. We become His hands and feet on this earth.

Never forget that a warm hug from your own two arms may be the touch of God someone desperately needs today. Don't hold back. God may be using you to answer someone's heartfelt prayer.

NEVER WALK AWAY FROM SOMEONE WHO DESERVES
HELP; YOUR HAND IS GOD'S HAND FOR THAT PERSON.
PROVERBS 3:27 MSG

83.
God has pursued you throughout your life.

Imagine a love story where a prince falls in love with a heartless servant girl. She lies to him. She berates him in front of the royal court. She runs around with other men, flaunting her tawdry relationships before the prince's very eyes. She enjoys the bounty of the prince's food and finery without so much as one word of thanks, more interested in the gifts than in the giver himself.

Though his love is continually rebuffed, the prince refuses to give up on the girl. When she breaks the rules of the kingdom, he not only forgives her, but he goes so far as to accept her punishment as his own. His advisors question the prince's seemingly misguided love, but he sees something they don't—the wonderful woman this servant girl was created to be.

Male or female, we're all that servant girl at heart. And we all have an infinitely loving, persistent Prince who has been wooing us since birth—regardless of how we've treated Him.

Take some time out today to consider how God has pursued you throughout your life. Think of how you've treated Him—the good, the bad, and the ugly.

Then reflect on how God has treated you. Spend a few moments thanking Him for the depth of His love for you.

GOD DEMONSTRATES HIS OWN LOVE TOWARD US,
IN THAT WHILE WE WERE YET SINNERS,
CHRIST DIED FOR US.
ROMANS 5:8 NASB

84.

You have the power to make evil run in the opposite direction.

"The devil made me do it!" is not a valid excuse for doing something you know wouldn't please God. The devil can't make you do anything. But you have the power to make the devil do something. You can make him hightail it and run.

All you have to do is say "yes" to God and "no" to evil. The choice is yours.

SUBMIT TO GOD. RESIST THE DEVIL
AND HE WILL FLEE FROM YOU.
JAMES 4:7 NKJV

85.
You will share in God's glory.

A close encounter with the living God made Moses' face shine, Isaiah shudder at the depth of his own depravity, and John fall at the Lord's feet as though he were dead. As God's children, we each have our own up-close-and-personal experience to look forward to the day we reach Heaven.

But there's no need for fear. First John 4:18 CEV reminds us that "perfect love drives fear away." In Heaven we'll come face-to-face with perfect love. We will also finally be close enough to God to not only reflect His glory but to enter into it, to share it, to revel in it. That's cause for celebration—and anticipation.

BECAUSE OF OUR LORD JESUS CHRIST, WE LIVE AT PEACE WITH GOD. CHRIST HAS ALSO INTRODUCED US TO GOD'S UNDESERVED KINDNESS ON WHICH WE TAKE OUR STAND. SO WE ARE HAPPY, AS WE LOOK FORWARD TO SHARING IN THE GLORY OF GOD.
ROMANS 5:1-2 CEV

86.
You are dust.

It's true that God cherishes you. Even before you were formed in your mother's womb, God treasured the very thought of you. He made special plans for you. One of those plans was that you would spend eternity by His side, where He could continue to nurture you and lavish His love on you. To God, no sacrifice was too great to assure this would happen, including having His Son leave His side and come to earth to die a painful death on your behalf.

Yes, you are of infinite worth in God's loving eyes. A beloved child cared for by an almighty Father. But, at the same time, another fact holds true. You are only dust. Without the touch of God's hand, without His life-giving breath, you would be worth no more than a grain of sand at the seashore or a speck of dust ready to be wiped off a shelf. Without God, you would be totally worthless, and lifeless, instead of eternally priceless.

Holding on to these two truths at the same time gives you a true picture of who you are. Without God's intervention you are literally nothing; but once God gets involved in your life, your worth to Him and to the world is literally unfathomable, because it is so great. Hold tightly to both truths. Take time to thank God for His role in your life and your worth.

AS A FATHER HAS COMPASSION ON HIS CHILDREN, SO THE LORD HAS COMPASSION ON THOSE WHO FEAR HIM; FOR HE KNOWS HOW WE ARE FORMED, HE REMEMBERS THAT WE ARE DUST.
PSALM 103:13–14 NIV

87.
You are part of God's family.

The word "family" often conjures up an image of a station wagon filled with emotional baggage. For some people, these emotions are positive. To them, "family" brings to mind happy memories, a sense of security, belonging, and unconditional love. For others, the word may ring hollow, coldly echoing broken promises, unmet expectations, or even abandonment.

Whatever your personal family experience, once you become a child of God you not only bond with your Heavenly Father, but you gain a brand-new family. And these familial relations are eternal.

These two families also have something in common—other than simply being related to you. They are both made up of imperfect people. People who will try and fail. People who are bound to make mistakes as they mature. People you may delight in, disagree with, or even wholeheartedly dislike. People who at times will overwhelm your life with love. People who may wound you more deeply than you thought possible. People who, if the truth be told, are probably a lot like you.

Every one of these people is someone God dearly loves. God longs for you to love each of them as well.

That's where the tricky part comes in. It's easy to love people you like. But true love goes far deeper. It reaches out even when someone else refuses to reach back.

There is no way to practice love other than to spend time with people. That's probably one reason God designed the concept of family in the first place. While all relationships have their own challenges, building relationships within God's family also has unparalleled rewards. Within the context of your church family, both local and universal, you can discover the joy of acceptance, encouragement, spiritual and physical support, comfort, and accountability. You can join your heart with others who love God like you do, as you work and worship together. As you grow closer to one another, you can help each other grow closer to God.

It is love that first made you part of God's family. As you risk reaching out to others with that same unconditional love, you can help make the word family one of the most wonderful words in your vocabulary.

LOVE YOUR SPIRITUAL FAMILY.
1 PETER 2:17 MSG

88.
Your purpose in life will be fulfilled.

In the Old Testament, God wanted the Israelites to thrive in a "promised land" where they could freely worship Him. A lot of obstacles threatened to keep this from happening . . . Pharaoh, Moses' fear of public speaking, the Egyptian army, the barrier of the Red Sea, the Israelites' own propensity toward idol worship, rumors of giants, and a trip through the desert that ran forty years too long. But eventually God's purposes were fulfilled, in spite of everything the Israelites faced.

What obstacles hinder God's unique purpose for your life? What fears, difficulties, or personal weaknesses make up your own Red Sea? God still has the power to part the proverbial waves and allow you to cross to the other side on dry land. But you are the one who has to do the walking.

God will fulfill His purpose whether you choose to follow Him or not. But why "wander in the desert" for forty years if you don't have to? The Promised Land of God's good purpose awaits. All you need to do to assure a timely arrival is stay close to God. Choose to do what He asks, even if it seems hard or you don't fully understand all the "whys." Continue to move forward, choosing to grow in your relationship with God by studying His Word and reaching out to others with His love. Then keep your eyes open. The Red Sea could part at any moment.

✠

THE LORD WILL FULFILL HIS PURPOSE FOR ME.
PSALM 138:8 NIV

89.
You can make the lives of those around you more flavorful.

Salt is rather common. Not much to look at. Fairly inexpensive. All in all, not something you spend much time thinking about. But salt is important to life. Your body needs it. Bland food tastes better with a sprinkle of it. It acts as a natural preservative. (Think beef jerky.) And salt can make you thirsty if you get enough of it.

Jesus compared those who followed Him—that includes you—with salt. Think about it. When you share God's love and His promise of eternal life with others, you offer them a "better-tasting life," one where bitterness can be transformed into something worth savoring. You make them thirsty to know more about God and help point them toward God's natural preservative—eternal life.

Through you, a little sprinkle of God's love can go a long way.

JESUS SAID, "YOU ARE LIKE SALT
FOR EVERYONE ON EARTH."
MATTHEW 5:13 CEV

90.
Every wrong you've ever done has been forgiven.

Suppose you were betrayed by a close friend. Someone you trusted. Someone you loved. Someone who made a conscious decision to hurt you more deeply than you thought possible.

How easy would it be to offer unconditional forgiveness? To completely let go of every ounce of bitterness or stray thought about getting even? Sounds like a tough order. Yet God fills it every day. At its heart, every sin is an act of betrayal. It is rebellion against a Father who deeply loves you. And every sin, no matter how big or small, builds a barrier between you and a perfectly holy God.

You can't knock that barrier down with remorse, denial, or even repentance. The only thing strong enough to remove it is the gift of God's grace. Although Jesus paid for this gift of grace with His life, God does not hold that against you. He doesn't make you work to receive forgiveness. All you have to do is ask for it.

When you confess your rebellion, even if it feels like only a small indiscretion, what you are doing is agreeing with God that what you've done is wrong. When you ask for His forgiveness, you open the floodgates of His grace that have been unlocked by Christ's sacrifice. Any sign of your rebellious acts are washed away, completely and eternally.

God's grace guarantees there will be no future finger-pointing. His forgiveness is absolute. So you never need to tote around a load of guilt or keep confessing the same sin over and over again. God's given you a second chance—or even a third, fourth, or fiftieth. Your relationship is restored, cleansed, and whole once again.

THE LORD SAYS, "NO MATTER HOW DEEP THE STAIN OF YOUR SINS, I CAN REMOVE IT. I CAN MAKE YOU AS CLEAN AS FRESHLY FALLEN SNOW."
ISAIAH 1:18 NLT

91.
You are safe in God's care.

Life is filled with the threat of danger. All you have to do is read the morning paper to be reminded of what could happen to you today. But the paper doesn't tell the whole story. There is something, or more accurately "Someone," who is far more powerful than any cancer cell, drunk driver, or terrorist that may happen to cross your path.

God cares about you. He sees everything that happens to you. His angels fight for you. His plans for your life cannot be thwarted. No matter what dangers you may face, God is there, holding you safely in the palm of His loving hand. At times this place of safety may protect you physically and emotionally. But that is not always the case. God allows bad things to happen, even in the lives of those He loves. He allows natural consequences to take place. He allows death to close the door on this life so the gates of Heaven can be opened to welcome you into the next life.

Through it all you remain safe in God's care. Keeping in mind His presence, His plan, and His power can give you the courage to steady a fearful heart, the peace to maintain an eternal perspective, and the perseverance to keep moving forward, no matter how "unsafe" the road ahead may at first appear.

EVEN WHEN YOU ARE CHASED BY THOSE WHO SEEK
YOUR LIFE, YOU ARE SAFE IN THE CARE OF THE LORD
YOUR GOD, SECURE IN HIS TREASURE POUCH!
1 SAMUEL 25:29 NLT

92.
Your thoughts have a powerful impact.

You can look like a saint on the outside and yet harbor a murderer's heart. Amazing, but Jesus said it was true. In Matthew 5:21–22 MSG, Jesus said, "You're familiar with the command to the ancients, 'Do not murder.' I'm telling you that anyone who is so much as angry with a brother or sister is guilty of murder."

Ouch. That hits close to home. But keeping in mind our potential for both life-giving love and homicidal hate does several things. It keeps us humble. It encourages us to take our thoughts seriously so that when our mind starts leading us away from God we can get back on the right track. It encourages us to resolve conflict quickly, preventing bitterness from growing in our hearts. And it reminds us how impossible it is to live a truly "good" life on our own. Only with God's help can our lives be characterized by love, both inside and out.

ANYONE WHO HATES ANOTHER CHRISTIAN
IS REALLY A MURDERER AT HEART.
1 JOHN 3:15 NLT

93.
Your heart will last forever.

You were made for more . . . more than landing a good job, building a few close relationships, keeping a clean credit rating, maybe raising a couple of kids, and even for more than making your unique mark on history. You were made to spend eternity in the company of a loving God.

Your heart knows this is true. Even before you first reached out to God, your heart whispered, "There's more to life than this." Don't try to drown out that whisper. The discontent and disillusionment you feel is not always born out of a selfish desire for the "good life." After all, your heart was made for the good life, a life of love that never ends. But so far you've had only a mere taste of that life, an appetizer of what's to come. Savor it. But listen to your heart. The best truly is yet to come.

HE HAS PLANTED ETERNITY IN THE HUMAN HEART, BUT EVEN SO, PEOPLE CANNOT SEE THE WHOLE SCOPE OF GOD'S WORK FROM BEGINNING TO END.
ECCLESIASTES 3:11 NLT

94.
You can harvest a crop of love.

Doing the right thing does more than benefit others and delight God. It also allows God's love to bloom more abundantly in your own heart. If you want to feel God's love more deeply, then follow Him more closely. By doing what pleases Him, you'll make your own life more beautiful.

PLANT THE GOOD SEEDS OF RIGHTEOUSNESS
AND YOU WILL REAP A CROP OF MY LOVE; PLOW THE
HARD GROUND OF YOUR HEARTS, FOR NOW
IS THE TIME TO SEEK THE LORD.
HOSEA 10:12 TLB

95.
You are delightful to God.

A string of joyously repeated chords echoes from the organ toward the rafters. Everyone stands, craning their necks toward the back of the church for their very first glimpse. The bride is making an entrance.

Yet one glance at the groom's face is all anyone needs to understand what's most important about the woman making her way down the church aisle. This woman is loved. Just her presence, and the promise of spending life together, fills her beloved with visible delight. No wonder weddings are such a cause for celebration.

This kind of celebration is being prepared for you. God is waiting for your arrival in Heaven like a groom awaits the entrance of his bride. You are the object of that once-in-a-lifetime kind of love, of a commitment that goes far deeper than any earthly marriage covenant ever could. It's true that God's love isn't exclusive. God loves countless others beside you. Yet this does nothing to diminish the unique love relationship He has with you.

You are not simply one of a "harem." You are an

individual; God's face lights up when He looks at you. No one can take your place in His heart. As you continue to fall more in love with Him while you're here on earth, your longing to please Him will grow, just as it does with any couple in love. In that way, you can give God cause to rejoice over you right now—even before you meet Him in Heaven.

Consider ways you can delight God today. (Hint: Just taking a moment out to tell Him how much you love Him is an excellent start!)

GOD WILL REJOICE OVER YOU AS
A BRIDEGROOM WITH HIS BRIDE.
ISAIAH 62:5 TLB

96.
When you help others you also help yourself.

Want to do yourself a favor? Lend a hand to someone else. When you see a need, ask God if there is something you should do to fill it. Then take action. You'll find that giving of yourself doesn't leave you with less. Instead, it enhances your life with love and unexpected blessings.

THE ONE WHO BLESSES OTHERS IS ABUNDANTLY
BLESSED; THOSE WHO HELP OTHERS ARE HELPED.
PROVERBS 11:25 MSG

97.
You are perfect.

This doesn't sound possible. After all, you're human. You make mistakes. You make bad choices. You know you're not able to live up to the holy standard that God requires to share an eternal relationship with Him. That's why you need Jesus, right?

That's true. But Jesus did more than open the door for you to enter Heaven. He made you perfect in God's eyes today, tomorrow, and throughout eternity.

WITH ONE SACRIFICE HE [CHRIST] MADE PERFECT
FOREVER THOSE WHO ARE BEING MADE HOLY.
HEBREWS 10:14 NCV

98.
Heaven, not earth, is your true home.

A foreigner is someone who calls another country "home." Someone who may look different, follow different customs, even speak a different language.

God says that you are a foreigner. Your driver's license and passport may state that you're right at home, but the Bible says that you're far from it. You're really a citizen of Heaven.

That's why those who follow God never really "fit" in down here. They were never meant to. They are refugees who will truly be home only when they are with God.

If you find yourself comfortable in today's society, if you don't stand out in a crowd as someone whose goals, values, and actions are foreign, you may want to take a good look at your life. Are you trying to make yourself at home in this world, or are you staying true to your citizenship in Heaven?

OUR CITIZENSHIP IS IN HEAVEN.
PHILIPPIANS 3:20 NKJV

99.
Your future is not in your hands.

You can plan ahead. You can invest in a 401K and your company's retirement program. You can work out and eat right. You can lay out goals for the future and take active steps to meet these objectives in a timely fashion. You can do everything "right" to get where you want to go. But the truth is that no one knows what the future holds—no one except God.

Your future is in God's hands, not your own. Keeping this truth in mind helps you maintain a realistic view of tomorrow. It doesn't alleviate you of the responsibility of doing your best to move in the direction you believe God wants you to go, but it does let you relax once you've done your best. The rest is up to God.

I AM TRUSTING YOU, O LORD, SAYING, "YOU ARE MY GOD!" MY FUTURE IS IN YOUR HANDS.
PSALM 31:14–15 NLT

100.
You are a living work of art.

The word "masterpiece" isn't a label to be tossed around lightly. It brings to mind names like Van Gogh, da Vinci, Renoir, and Michelangelo. Each of these men were "masters," well known for their creative genius in their field. Their works surpassed common craftsmanship, reaching a pinnacle of perfection seemingly out of reach of their peers. Each original "masterpiece" is irreplaceable, possessing an artistic excellence and a unique beauty that made it priceless.

You are a masterpiece created by the greatest artist who ever was or ever will be. Your inestimable worth and beauty were determined the moment you were created by His omnipotent, creative hand. Irreplaceable, unique, and of incalculable worth, you are something to be treasured. No one hides a masterpiece in the cellar or mounts it with a staple gun. It's meticulously cared for and put in a position where it can bring the most joy to the greatest number of people.

Never forget that you are more than just a bunch of cells that happen to be working together. You are God's masterpiece. Don't allow your own weaknesses or the criticism of others to dim the truth of who God created you to be. Not all masterpieces are recognized as such by their peers. Sometimes it takes years for others to appreciate their true beauty. But that doesn't mean it wasn't there in the first place.

Learn to see yourself for who you really are—a living work of art.

WE ARE GOD'S MASTERPIECE.
EPHESIANS 2:10 NLT

101.
Life will never be too much for you to handle— with God's help.

There's a pithy little saying that is often repeated when people are facing hard times: God will never give you more than you can handle. Sounds good. Sounds true. Sounds exactly like what a loving God would do. But the problem with this saying is that it doesn't tell the whole truth—the true-to-life, day-by-day, honest-to-goodness-reality-of-life truth.

As a matter of fact, it could be said that the exact opposite of this adage is true. God will continually give you more than you can handle. You may face relational problems that seem irreparable. Financial disaster. Terminal illness. Destructive habits you just can't seem to break. The continual pull to do things you know are contrary to God's desire for your life. And ultimately you will come face-to-face with death.

More than you can handle? You bet. On your own, that is. Only by relying on God can you not only handle, but also have victory over, the hard times you will face in this life. First Corinthians 10:13 MSG, says "All you need to remember is that God will never let you down; he'll never let you be pushed past your limit; he'll always be there to help you come through it."

That's the whole truth. Life will always be more than you can handle. But you have a loving Father who never leaves your side. An all-powerful King whose help is only a prayer away.

Turn to Him. Not only for help, but just because you love Him. Then go out there and face life. Together, you can handle anything.

BE PREPARED. YOU'RE UP AGAINST FAR MORE THAN
YOU CAN HANDLE ON YOUR OWN.
EPHESIANS 6:13 MSG

Bible Acknowlegments